Resilience

Social Skills
for Effective Learning
Volume 2

Annie Greeff

Crown House Publishing Limited
www.crownhouse.co.uk

Published by

Crown House Publishing Ltd
Crown Buildings, Bancyfelin, Carmarthen, Wales, SA33 5ND, UK
www.crownhouse.co.uk

and

Crown House Publishing Company LLC
4 Berkeley Street, 1st Floor, Norwalk, CT 06850, USA
www.CHPUS.com

British Library of Cataloguing-in-Publication Data
A catalogue entry for this book is available from the British Library.

International Standard Book Number 1904424643

Library of Congress Control Number 2004111625

Project management: Janice Baiton Editorial Services, Cambridge
Cover design: Tom Fitton, Crown House Publishing
Text design: Paul Barrett Book Production, Cambridge
Typesetting: Jean Cussons, Diss, Norfolk
Printed and bound in the UK by
Cromwell Press, Trowbridge, Wiltshire

Contents

Foreword

When we choose to work with children, we do it in the hope that we prepare them for a happy, productive and fulfilling adult life. In our uncertainty about what the future may hold, we strive to equip them with all the skills they could need. It is with pride and gratitude that we observe them when they achieve success, or make the right decisions, but ultimately what we really want to see is that they find happiness and meaning in life while they enjoy the love and care of others.

It has been said that no one can rightfully claim to be a self-made person. Each successful person was given opportunities, encouragement, support, love, feedback or even hard times that facilitated growth and development in a certain direction. If we truly believe in a purpose-driven life, we have to acknowledge that an individual's purpose is linked to service to others, in some form or another. Through refined interpersonal skills, it is simply much easier to connect with others, in order to contribute to their lives.

We live in a world that consists of various formal and informal groups and functional teams, the success and happiness of which depend on the ability of the members to make their relationships work so well that they can concentrate on getting the job done. In a broader context, our sensitivity towards others and their needs affect global relationships. To ensure peaceful co-existence we need to actively work at relationships, common understanding and mutual respect. This mindset of being actively engaged in life, yet being flexible enough to allow for differences, is fundamental to social resilience.

Annie Greeff
January 2005

Using this book

Resilience Volumes 1 and 2 is designed to facilitate the mastery of personal and social skills needed to be an effective learner. To assist the teacher in the facilitation of the learning process, the author has included the formal theory related to the topic, based on research and practical experience. To simplify the transfer of the knowledge and skills to children, *Resilience* contains guidelines to the teacher and activities for child participation.

Thus each volume contains an introduction and a series of units covering personal (Volume 1) or social (Volume 2) skills. Each unit comprises a theoretical introduction or broad overview of the topic, followed by guidelines for the teacher and activity sheets for the children.

Guidelines include:

- *Learning points* to clarify the aim or main purpose of the activity.
- *Comments* to guide the process and supply practical advice or potential responses where applicable.
- *Tips* to support the teacher in the presentation of the contents.
- *Timing* to indicate the approximate duration of instructions, activities and conclusion.

Activity sheets are:

- designed to structure the experiential learning process.
- photocopiable for use by the children.

At the end of each unit, the Action Plan:

- summarizes the learning related to the topic.
- revises main learning points.
- acts as a stimulus for changes in behaviour or the strengthening/support of existing good habits.

May you and the children you teach experience great satisfaction, personal growth and a sense of purpose through the use of these volumes. Enjoy the journey!

Acknowledgements

Thank you to the many people who contributed to my understanding of social skills and the creation of this book:

My family for love, laughter and support.

My friend Adri for believing in me and encouraging me to venture out.

My colleagues Madel, Helene, Melodie, and Lillian for reminding me of what I am capable of.

My clients for trusting me and challenging me to make a difference.

Everybody at Crown House Publishing for each contributing in their special way: Helen Kinsey for seeing potential in the workbook; Bill Lucas for valuable guidance and feedback; David Bowman for giving me this opportunity; Karen Bowman for handling important paperwork; Tom Fitton for creating and recreating the cover design; Rosalie Williams for handling reviews; and those who worked behind the scenes for turning my manuscript into this book.

Janice Baiton for managing this enormous project.

Finally, I am grateful to my Creator for so many gifts.

Introduction

Outline

Introduction

Developing social competencies

Today, many families live in neighbourhoods where they are afraid to let children play outside. The result is that children spend hours watching videos or TV, sending text messages or playing with a computer. Children and their parents spend less time talking to each other or visiting relatives and neighbours. Previously, these interactions were the opportunities to learn emotional skills. Now we have to find alternative methods of teaching such skills to children. The school is probably a good place to start this process, and this means that teachers will have to fulfil the roles of life coaches. What is being measured most of the time is the academic part of the curriculum, therefore the attention to cognitive or thinking skills is at the expense of emotional skills. With the strong emphasis on academic success, it requires a definite change in mindset to address emotional skills.

Paul Hawken (quoted in Crane, 2000) said:

> We lead by being human. We do not lead by being corporate, by being professional or by being institutional.

In modern leadership, the leader is required to role model lifelong learning and continuous personal growth. Modern leadership implies a certain level of vulnerability, which is a result of connecting with others on a more personal level, and admitting one's own mistakes and weaknesses. The extent to which we share information about ourselves depends on the level of trust in our relationship, and requires good judgement and timing.

When working with children through the use of this book, it may be the only time during a whole day or even week that some individuals will receive focused attention. Whatever the reasons may be, many families do not have regular, constructive, high-quality family interaction. Where else could young people learn or reinforce emotional competencies, if it does not happen at home?

During the work sessions on resilience, children will be listened to and have the opportunity to express their concerns and emotions in a safe environment. When young people are more in touch and in control of their emotions, and acknowledge other people's emotions, teachers may actually reap the benefits in their classrooms! Thomas Peters and Robert Waterman (1982) said:

> The simple act of paying positive attention to people has a great deal to do with productivity.

A caring relationship with a teacher gives children the motivation for wanting to succeed.

By being a caring person, the teacher acts as a role model in forming caring relationships. Most parents were not trained in emotional competencies, and traditional teacher training did not include the refinement of such skills either. However, a favourite teacher is not just an instructor for academic skills but also a confidant and becomes an inspiring role model for caring relationships.

Although it would be unreasonable to expect teachers who are already carrying a heavy work burden to also become counsellors and confidants, their influence on children's lives is indisputable. However, working with children with the purpose of developing personal and social skills will spark personal growth in both directions.

> Real education consists of drawing the best out of yourself.
>
> *Mahatma Ghandi*

Teachers as emotional caretakers

Ron Edmonds (1986), the so-called grandfather of school effectiveness research, wrote:

> A school can create a coherent environment so potent that for at least six hours a day it can override almost everything else in the lives of children.

Every child needs encouragement, acknowledgement and acceptance. It is amazing how many successful employees can identify at least one supportive or inspiring person who played a significant role in their personal or career development. So, too, will most people remember a special teacher who paid attention, conveyed high expectations and recognized inputs and successes.

As an investor in people, you have the power to build the self-esteem of a child. Teachers do not always get the public recognition for their work with children, and are often on the receiving end when it comes to criticism. However, by being personally involved in the development of a young person, you earn a place in the heart and life of a human being.

In leadership models, parenting and teaching, it is general knowledge that role modelling is the most effective way of changing people. Some educationalists believed that role modelling may not be the best way to teach – it may be the only way to teach! The actions of a role model are very powerful in bringing about a desired behaviour because actions do speak louder than words. However, the ideal role model is not a perfect being. Modern leadership is not synonymous with perfection – leaders can make mistakes and show their emotions. When they admit mistakes, they become more 'human' and people can associate with them. Young people can associate with less than perfect leaders. More important than anything else is for young people to know that they are loved and that somebody is there for them. Love in this context means unconditional acceptance of the person. You may not always agree with the actions and behaviours of children, but you can accept them

as people. The most beloved modern leaders seem to be vulnerable and less than perfect. It is their warmth and caring nature that gives them a place in people's hearts.

When you work through this resource book, you will possibly embark on your own personal development journey as you rethink some of your own beliefs, values and actions. In this process of personal growth, you will demonstrate the healthy habits of lifelong learning and flexible thinking.

While the news emphasizes the darker side of life – corruption, murder, HIV Aids pandemic, the gap in the ozone layer, war, unrest, the list goes on – it creates a frame of reference in the minds of children. Different generations have different frames of reference, and therefore respond differently to challenges. How do you balance hope and a positive outlook on the future with a bleak reality? How do you inspire young people to believe in the future when their own personal realities may be anything but bright?

Your biggest challenge is possibly to start believing in a bright future yourself. So, before you embark on this personal journey with children, ask yourself:

- What do I believe about myself?
- What do I believe about children?
- What do I believe about the future?

Your beliefs create your reality. Your beliefs become your self-fulfilling prophesy. And your beliefs about children determine where you take them during this journey.

Teachers as facilitators

Facilitating a typical work session

Facilitation

Facilitation in this context means non-directive guidance of a learning process. It is different from normal teaching. The emphasis is on asking the right questions and providing the right activities to enable young people to see for themselves what the possible results of changing behaviour or expanding behaviour patterns could be. Facilitation is therefore different from teaching, preaching, testing, telling, directing, lecturing, mentoring, coaching, counselling and leading.

Experiential learning, role play and games

Experiential learning means literally learning from experiencing the activity and reflecting on what was learned. It is not about listening to the expert but rather about simulating real-life situations, role playing, and participating in games.

In conventional schooling, the main focus is on the development of the mind. In experiential learning, the body, mind, thoughts, feelings and actions are involved. Experiential learning is therefore whole-person learning.

Group work and sharing ideas

Group work is vital for active participation and sharing. Most exercises are designed for small group activities, with feedback to the larger (whole) group. Active group participation promotes the learning of new skills, new attitudes and new knowledge about individuals as well as group dynamics.

The principle that 'none of us is as smart as all of us' becomes particularly evident in group learning. While group learning stimulates the refinement of group skills as basic life skills, great care should be taken to balance democratic facilitation, experiential learning and reflection.

It should be made clear that sharing is never forced and respect for privacy is encouraged, especially when some people may experience difficulty and feel sensitive about issues.

Reflection

Reflective activities may include individual reflection or group discussions aimed at integrating the learning process into existing frames of knowledge. This is done by observing, recapturing and evaluating the experience in an atmosphere of mutual respect and support. Although the activity sheets in this book are designed to simplify this process, children should also be encouraged to keep personal journals for further reflection and lasting learning.

Format of a typical learning session

Breaking the ice

The aim is to familiarize the children with the topic or main theme of the unit. Activities could take the format of fun exercises, movement, dancing, role plays or reflection.

Connecting to the self

This can be any exercise that allows the children to connect to personal experiences and existing frames of reference or understanding of the issue. Self-assessments are useful for this purpose.

Sharing with others

Creating an opportunity to discuss personal viewpoints as discovered/affirmed in the 'Connecting to the self' exercise.

Taking part in activities

An activity that enables the thorough exploration of the main theme. It should involve all participants in experiential learning, either in the format of individual exercises or in a group context.

Giving and receiving feedback

Group sharing and formulating summarized responses of individuals or groups enable the larger group to share viewpoints. This could also include brainstorming sessions.

Reflecting

This covers learning from experience, own and others' opinions, and integrating the information into existing personal frameworks. It is about the expression of personal opinions and feelings and the application of knowledge and insights.

Making notes

Throughout the work session, notes could be made and displayed on a board or on sheets of paper. These would be the comments made by the participants and should be in their own words. Notes could also include analysis, summaries or conclusions and learning points.

Evaluating

By asking children which activities worked and what they did not enjoy or view as useful, the teacher is able to improve or expand on certain aspects of the workshop. Encouraging young people to give feedback demonstrates mutual respect, invites participation and ownership, and develops communication skills through the clear, tactful expression of personal opinions.

Empathy

I care

Outline

Outcomes

On completion of this unit, children should have the necessary knowledge, skills and attitudes to recognize and acknowledge their own and other people's emotions. They should be able to:

- notice and understand their own emotions.

- understand what caused their emotions.

- notice others' emotions.

- acknowledge other people's emotions.

- interpret others' emotions.

- read and interpret body language.

- listen for facts, opinions and feelings.

- show that they are listening.

- keep on refining listening skills.

- share emotions (talk about them).

> Children who experience being loved and accepted as they are,
> who do not feel their basic worth is continually on trial
> in their parents' eyes, have a priceless advantage in the
> formation of healthy self-esteem.
>
> *Nathaniel Branden (1994)*

Overview

The Cassell Compact Dictionary defines empathy as 'the capacity for identifying with the experience of others, or appreciating things or emotions outside ourselves'. Empathy is about objectively acknowledging another person's feelings. It does not mean that you fully understand or agree, but rather that you take notice in a respectful way.

Empathy is different from sympathy, which is defined as 'the quality of being affected with the same feelings as another person or of sharing emotions, affections, inclinations, etc. with another person'. At a glance, sympathy seems to be similar to owning the same feeling as the other person.

If empathy is stepping into the other person's shoes, sympathy is stepping into the shoes and feeling the same way about those shoes as the owner does! If sympathy is like co-owning the other person's load, it could make you, as the listener, less effective and maybe too subjective to keep perspective.

In reality, a common need is to be acknowledged – you want others to pay attention, not to take over your burden. Therefore a typical comment is: 'I don't want your sympathy. I just want you to listen.'

Empathy – unconditional love?

Al Siebert (1996), a well-known psychologist investigating the field of resilience, wrote that highly resilient individuals have a need beyond Abraham Maslow's hierarchy of basic needs (physiological, safety, love, self-esteem and self-actualization), namely, the need for synergy – the need that things should work out for you as well as for others. This need relates to empathy, caring and unconditional love. (And of course feeling good enough about yourself to be comfortable and unthreatened by others' success and good fortune.)

Walter Anderson (1997) wrote that a small child learns when to trust, an adolescent finds his own identity, and a mature person looks beyond himself. In other words, a mature person demonstrates emotional interest that goes beyond selfish personal needs and includes the concerns, well-being and happiness of others.

In his book *How to Get What You Want and Want What You Have*, John Gray (1999) refers to 'love tanks' and links them to different life stages. These love tanks could be compared to the well-known Life Stages theory formulated by Edgar Schein in 1978. According to both theories, certain relationships and thus certain types of love are more in the foreground during certain life stages. But as Gray writes, you need to keep all love tanks filled to stay young and retain your zest for life!

Tank	Age	Love need
Tank 1	Conception to birth	Love and support of the Creator
Tank 2	0-7 years	Parent's love and support
Tank 3	7–14 years	Love and support from family and friends, and having fun
Tank 4	14–21 years	Love and support from peers and others with similar goals
Tank 5	21–28 years	Self-love and support of yourself
Tank 6	28–35 years	Love and support from intimate relationships, partnerships and romance
Tank 7	35–42 years	Loving and supporting a dependant
Tank 8	42–49 years	Giving back to the community
Tank 9	49–56 years	Giving back to the world
Tank 10	56+ years	Serving God

The age groups in Gray's table are of course flexible and offer a helpful broad interpretation of psychological development stages and related emotional needs. However, it is interesting that up to age 21, love tanks are about getting (receiving from others). The next phase seems to be a time of self-centredness (self-love) and after age 28 it is about giving (caring for and contributing towards others). Looking beyond yourself!

> There must be more to life than having everything.
>
> *Maurice Sendak*

Acceptance as a learning need

As a human being you want to be assured of your worth – others need to consider you as worthwhile and valuable enough to spend time hearing you out.

> I need to be seen
> I need to be heard
> I need to be respected
> I need to be safe
> I need to belong
> When all of my basic needs are met…
> then…
> I am ready to learn.
>
> *Anonymous*

Acknowledgement – to be truly heard, seen and accepted – is particularly relevant to the learning situation, whether at home or at school. A colleague once made the remark that when teenage pupils are most 'difficult', irritating and exhausting than ever, they are screaming for empathy – harder than ever!

> When I truly hear a person and the meanings that are important to him at that moment, hearing not simply his words, but him, and when I let him know that I have heard his own private personal meanings, many things happen. There is first of all a grateful look. He feels released. He wants to tell me more about his world.

He surges forth in a new sense of freedom. I think he becomes more open to the process of change.

> *Carl Rogers quoted in David Ryback (1998)*

This empathy and compassion with others relates to love as an act of unconditional acceptance. Many will agree that love is also the answer to healing of any kind. John Gray (1999) wrote:

> When we heal the pain of others as we give them compassion, our own inner pain has a chance to come up and is sometimes automatically released.

Developing empathic future leaders

Being a professional implies that you act correctly, even if you do not feel like it at the time. It requires self-control, gut-feelings and self/internal motivation, in addition to being aware of your own and others' feelings without being overwhelmed and swept along with them.

Many experts in the field of leadership development agree that business leaders who are capable of noticing, evaluating and expressing emotion will be more in demand. In the new world of business, leadership is business oriented without being mechanistic, and caring without being soppy.

Managers with empathy are able to make people feel at ease. They create opportunities for sharing and participation. Outstanding leaders probably became leaders because they could manage well, but management is an entry-level set of skills. Leadership includes emotional competencies. Personally I view leadership as an advanced application of emotional competencies, of which showing empathy is one.

Workplace stress leads to absenteeism. Bottled-up emotions, interpersonal differences, feelings of helplessness, overwork and imbalances in life-style are just some of the workplace hazards that can overwhelm you. To successfully navigate through the minefield of emotional upsets in the workplace, you need to lead with empathy and emotional skill.

Helping people better manage upsetting feelings – anger, anxiety, depression, pessimism and loneliness – is a form of disease prevention.

Daniel Goleman (1998)

	Listening	Speaking	Reading	Writing
Order learnt	First	Second	Third	Fourth
Extent used	45%	30%	16%	9%
	Most	Second most	Second least	Least
Taught in school	Least	Seldom	Next most	Most

Communicate to connect

The exciting thing to note is that the key to power today is available to us all. If you weren't a king in medieval times, you might have had a great deal of difficulty becoming one. If you didn't have capital at the beginning of the industrial revolution, the odds of your amassing it seemed very slim indeed. But today, any kid in blue jeans can create a corporation that can change the world. In the modern world information is the commodity of kings. Those with access to certain forms of specialized knowledge can transform themselves and, in many ways, our entire world.

Anthony Robbins (1992)

Yet, if communication is so important, how well do you communicate on an interpersonal level and what are the most relevant communication skills to use in different situations?

The following table by Courtland and Thill (1992) demonstrates the relationship between different communication skills and their progressive development.

Although we use listening skills 45 per cent of the time, it seems to be the skill taught the least in school. This makes the training of listening skills, especially empathic listening, a necessity in any kind of personal or interpersonal development course.

Types of listening

Different situations require different listening skills. These vary not only in purpose, but also in the amount of emotional involvement, level of interaction and extent to which feedback is given.

Listening for enjoyment

This type of listening takes place when you listen to music, watch a film or enjoy casual conversation. The purpose is amusement and relaxation.

Listening for facts

The goal for this type of listening is to understand and retain factual information. You have to identify the key points in the message and question, check or judge accuracy.

Situation	Skills needed
When things are going well – we are OK.	Our **overall communication** may be OK and easy-going.
When I feel unhappy about another person's behaviour.	I assert myself and give **feedback** using a WIN message.
When another person has a problem or concern.	I **listen** to understand, asking questions for better understanding.
When both of us have a concern.	We do **conflict management** using a toolkit of communication skills, problem-solving skills and negotiation skills.

Listening for meaning

For critical listening, the goal is to evaluate the message at many levels: the logic of the argument; the strength and reliability of the evidence; the validity of what has been conveyed; the credibility and implications of the communication; and the intentions of the speaker.

Listening for emotions

Empathic listening is about acknowledging the emotions, needs and wants of the speaker so that you can appreciate that person's reality regardless of your own perspective. It requires an unbiased, open mind and the willingness to accept the other person's reality and spend time hearing the person out. This is probably one of the most challenging skills to master, and it would be unrealistic to expect immediate results when teaching empathic listening skills.

If we are perfectly honest with ourselves, we would realize that most of us are more likely to listen to others not in order to understand their reality, but to judge how right or wrong they are compared to what we consider to be the truth.

When you are judgemental in your approach to people, you are unlikely to listen with empathy. When you listen with empathy, you listen with an open mind, focusing on the other person's concerns, not your own.

Preparing to listen for understanding

It has been said that no person could truly and fully understand another person's life or emotions, because as a human being you only understand what you have personally experienced. If that is true, you can try doing the next best thing: listening to acknowledge – whether you understand or not! The following guidelines could help people in general to be more effective at empathic listening.

1 *Right mindset* – Not all people are natural counsellors, but there are times when empathic listening skills are really helpful. Empathic listening

promotes trusting relationships. However, mental preparation is important. Empathic listening is not about giving advice, criticism or coaching. The challenge is to listen with an open mind, not so much to gather factual information but rather to hear the emotion behind the words.

2 *Right time* – Agree on a suitable time to hear the person out. Listening takes time. If you are pressed for time, make an appointment for a period when you are free from other commitments. It may feel rude to postpone this conversation but it is certainly less rude than only half-listening with your mind pre-occupied with other thoughts or urgent tasks.

3 *Right place* – Choose a private place that is convenient and comfortable for both of you. Give attention to the physical setting – it is better to sit at a 90 degree angle (not facing each other directly) without a physical barrier, like a table, between the two of you. Make sure that the place you chose will allow you to be free from interruptions. When a person shares upsetting or intense emotions with you, it is damaging to the process to be interrupted.

Demonstrating that you listen

Some people are known for being good listeners but what are the typical, observable behaviours or actions that makes someone a good listener? The following pointers may be helpful.

Be quiet

Truly listening without interrupting encourages people to talk about what is bothering them. No one will be comfortable to share the details of personal troubles if you are doing most of the talking.

Respond without words

Silence alone does not fully demonstrate or ensure effective listening. Using different non-verbal responses such as eye contact, nodding your head, leaning forward and facial expressions such as smiling, help to show your attention. The so-called 'para language' responses such as 'Uh-huh' or 'mmm…' indicate that you are paying attention.

Encourage the person to venture further

People often need encouragement to go on or to explore deeper. Some examples are 'How do you feel about it?' 'Would you like to tell me more about that?' 'Do you want to talk about it?' Such open questions create the opportunity for the other person to expand and perhaps share more sensitive information.

Check for understanding

Reflective listening involves repeating to the speaker your understanding of what you have heard them say. This you do in your own words – your therefore rephrase the other person's words. By doing so you acknowledge another person's concerns and emotions.

Ask questions

Asking the right questions is crucial for getting the information you need. The following table offers a simplified summary of types of questions and typical examples.

Empathy and discipline

Some managers voice their concerns about showing empathy in the workplace because they do not comprehend how managers can be simultaneously caring yet firm. They think empathy means that people can 'get away with murder'. The whole issue of respect is in question here. In the workplace, empathy implies an understanding attitude while acknowledging the other person's accountability. It is about sharing and caring, but also about expecting commitment and good performance.

> Compassion and respect do not imply lack of firmness.
>
> *Nathaniel Branden (1994)*

When you have empathy with others, you are willing to listen with the intention of understanding their situation and how they feel about it. But, when you are accountable (as a manager or parent) you also need to ensure that rules are followed and tasks completed in an agreed manner. This responsibility requires that you clarify the boundaries of what is acceptable and what cannot be tolerated.

When subordinates or children do not conform to the agreed standards of performance, you have the

Types of questions	When to use	Example
Leading	Never	You don't understand that of course?
Multiple	Never	Why did you say that and what do you think you have achieved?
Probing	To check facts	What was the price per unit?
	To intervene	How did you start the process?
Specific	To focus vague or generalised statements	What specifically? In comparison to whom?
Restatement	To verify understanding of previous answers	You said that you find it difficult to complete the homework. Is that correct?
Reflective	To check for understanding of emotions	So you feel misunderstood?

Adapted from Bovée and Thill (1992) and IBM (1994)

responsibility to manage the situation. One way of managing it would be by reprimanding the person in question. You can also show your disappointment or frustration through your voice tone and facial expression, without being aggressive or making personal attacks. When your actions and intentions are aligned, you demonstrate congruence and people know where they stand with you, while they intuitively 'know' that you also have empathy with them.

A caring parent or manager is therefore able to balance empathy with objective decision-making and consistent firmness. In fact, true caring includes creating the security of clear boundaries. It is important to know what is acceptable, but equally important to know what is not.

You can be angry and still love and care. In the book *The One Minute Manager*, Blanchard and Johnson (2004) explain that until a person is fully trained for the task, it is not good practice to reprimand that person for mistakes on the job. In such cases incompetence is answered with coaching. But, when the person is task ready, the manager has the right to become angry and show anger. This is the time to reprimand – showing anger but not losing temper.

An experience of respect

Showing respect includes acknowledgement, dignity and positive regard. When you admire a person you look up to the person for being outstanding – a role model or inspiration. When you respect a person, you consider the person an equal. Somebody who is not more than you and not less than you – a human being that you honour as a human being, regardless of successes or failures.

> When pure sincerity forms within, it is outwardly realized in other people's hearts.
>
> *Lau Tsu (600 BC)*

> People are unreasonable, illogical, self-centered.
> Love them anyway.
> If you do good, people will accuse you of selfish, ulterior motives.
> Do good anyway.
> If you are successful, you will win false friends and true enemies.
> Try to be successful anyway.
> The good you do today will be forgotten tomorrow.
> Do it anyway.
> Honesty and frankness make you vulnerable.
> Be honest and frank anyway.
> What you spend years building may be destroyed overnight.
> Build anyway.
> People really need help, but they may attack you if you help them.
> Help them anyway.
> Give the world the best you have, and you'll get kicked in the teeth.
> Give the world the best you have anyway.
>
> *Karl Menninger (quoted in Crane, 2000)*

Guidelines
and
Activity Sheets

Guidelines: Activity Sheet 1

Noticing other people's emotions

Learning points

Noticing body language could be helpful in determining what another person is experiencing emotionally.

Comments

1 Instruct the group to work alone at first and then share with a learning partner.
2 Each pair assigns an emotion to each picture.
3 Pairs report back to the larger group.
4 Ask the group: 'Did you agree each time?'
5 Point out that interpretations could be different because people show emotions in their own unique way.

Tip

Ask three participants to stand in front of the group and, without using words, each to role play an emotion. You could either tell them which emotions to role play or leave it for them to decide.

The rest of the group has to guess which emotion they had in mind. There could be different interpretations.

Discuss the dangers of relying too heavily on body language without checking for accuracy.

Timing

2 minutes giving instructions

10 minutes pair work

3 minutes concluding

1 Noticing other people's emotions

👥 Share in pairs

1 Study the people in the pictures below and complete the phrase 'I feel …' for each person.
2 Share your opinion with a learning partner.
3 You have 10 minutes to both complete the game.

Guidelines: Activity Sheet 2

Sharing emotions

Learning points

Sharing the same emotions could be a binding factor in relationships. When you do not share the same emotions as the other person or group of people, it could make you feel excluded and lonely.

Comments

1 Pairs or groups of three discuss the pictures and write down their interpretations, with feedback to the larger group.
2 Ask the group: 'What are the dangers when many people get over excited or over emotional? What can go wrong?' Discuss historical events or events in newspapers when over-emotional reactions had adverse effects.

Tip

Ask the children about incidents during which many people feel the same emotions, such as great sports events, political events, music festivals, or religious events. Expand on the idea that emotions are 'contagious'. Our emotions affect other people around us.

Timing

5 minutes introduction

10 minutes group work

5 minutes concluding

2 Sharing emotions

👥 / 👥👥 Discussion

1 Look at the pictures of different groups of people below. Do they share the same emotions? Explain to the group what you see in each picture.
2 What happens when you do not have the same feelings as other people in your group?
3 Do you agree with the idea that emotions are 'contagious'? Explain your viewpoint to the group.

Guidelines: Activity Sheet 3

Noticing emotions in people close to me

Learning points

When family and friends are sensitive to each other's feelings, they are in a better position to form trusting relationships and feel safe with each other. This enhances resilience because experiences of social connection and cohesion depend on caring attitudes.

Comments

1 Instruct the children to be aware of the way in which other people show emotions, especially those close to them.
2 Notice how people show emotions in different ways.
3 This activity is best used for home play. If the children want to complete the form at home, they are welcome, otherwise verbal feedback will be enough. The feedback should be in the form of small group discussions during the next session.

Tip

Ask the group: 'Do you know a family in which all family members care about each other, talk to each other about the things they do during the day, and openly say how they feel? Describe that family and explain how they behave towards each other.'

Timing

5 minutes introduction

20 minutes small group discussions

5 minutes summarizing and concluding

3 Noticing emotions in people close to me

👤 Home play

What I notice about their body language and their behaviours…

	Mad	Sad	Glad	Scared
Mother				
Father				
Brother				
Sister				
Friend				
Other				

Guidelines: Activity Sheet 4

Noticing different emotions

Learning points

Being aware of emotions is a graded competency. Some people are highly sensitive to other people's feelings, they become too involved and almost take over the other person's emotions. Other people are insensitive, not feeling or caring at all. Both extremes are unhealthy. When you have empathy, you will be able to acknowledge and understand other people's emotions, while being objective enough to analyse the situation rationally or 'from a distance' at the same time. In this way you can evaluate circumstances accurately and form a balanced opinion.

Comments

1. Ask the children to rate themselves on the scale shown on Activity Sheet 4 based on how they think they react to other's feelings.
2. Talk about the story of Sarah who did not discuss her observations, but was deeply aware of other people and their preferences. It is worth noting that usually people who are very talkative are not so aware of other's feelings.

Timing

5 minutes introduction and Sarah's story

2 minutes self-rating

3 minutes concluding

4 Noticing different emotions

On your own

Read the text below and then decide what number you are on the empathy scale.

Cold fish
- Do not understand emotions
- Do not feel guilty when doing something wrong
- Do not work well with others
- Fight with others
- Hurt others
- Bully
- Tell lies

Warm teddy bear
- Comfortable with emotions
- Love others
- Enjoy working with others
- Make people feel good
- Repair friendships
- Try to be kind
- Want others to be happy

Soppy puppy
- Take over other people's problems
- Feel guilty when others suffer
- Talk about other people's problems all the time
- Want to be liked by everybody
- Cannot say no

Empathy scale

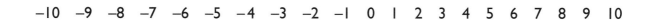

–10 –9 –8 –7 –6 –5 –4 –3 –2 –1 0 1 2 3 4 5 6 7 8 9 10

Large group

This is a story about Sarah, a quiet little girl in a playgroup. She often used to sit on her own, watching the others play. The teachers and her parents were a bit worried that she might have emotional problems.

Then one day, one of the teachers did an experiment. She asked each child in the class to explain to the rest of the class who played with whom, what the favourite games of the different groups of children were, and which toys they preferred to play with.

When it was Sarah's turn, everybody had a big surprise! She knew better than anybody else in the class what everybody else did or enjoyed the most.

Reflection

Where on the scale would you place Sarah?

Guidelines: Activity Sheet 5

Intuition

Learning points

It is human to sometimes inflate incidents or words out of proportion. Many misunderstandings and conflicts begin as small issues that are then overemphasized instead of being clarified. Discussing matters or asking what a person meant in the first place could save a lot of trouble. Assumptions are not the solution.

Comments

1 Discuss the diagram on Activity Sheet 5 and the meaning of gut feeling or intuition in the way you make judgements.
2 How often have you thought you knew what another person had in mind, when in fact you were wrong?
3 Intuition is useful, but should be checked for accuracy through tactful discussions and by asking good questions.

Timing

2 minutes introduction

5 minutes general discussion

3 minutes concluding

5 Intuition

👤 On your own

Have you ever experienced a situation when someone said something to you and, as time went by, you became more and more upset? For instance, Mary says: 'I don't like it when you talk so loud.' You find yourself becoming more and more upset.

What would be a wise thing to do when this happens?

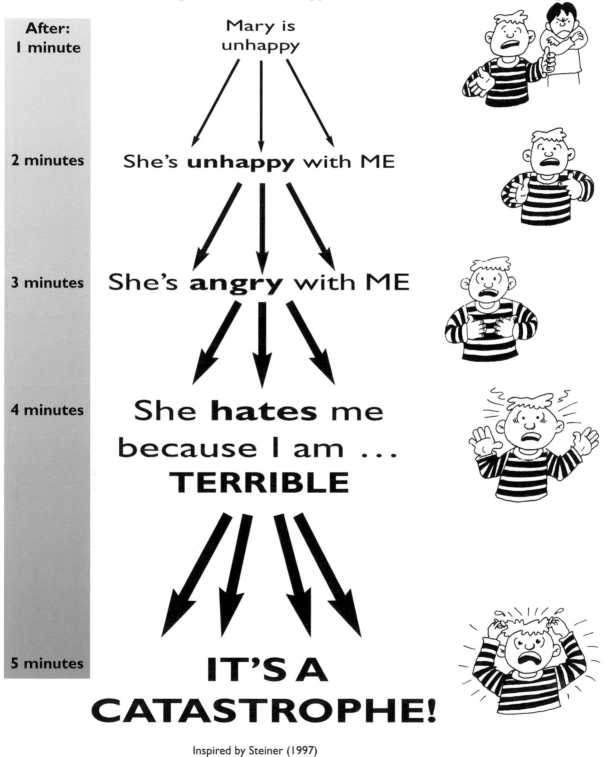

After:	
1 minute	Mary is unhappy
2 minutes	She's **unhappy** with ME
3 minutes	She's **angry** with ME
4 minutes	She **hates** me because I am ... TERRIBLE
5 minutes	IT'S A CATASTROPHE!

Inspired by Steiner (1997)

Guidelines: Activity Sheet 6

Questions

Learning points

Questioning is often an underrated communication skill. The quality of information you receive is related to the quality and type of question you ask. When planning to gather information, it is better to prepare the questions beforehand because asking too many questions can irritate others.

Comments

1 The children sit in pairs.
2 Each child prepares six questions related to the topic.
3 Each child gets the opportunity to ask questions and also to be questioned.
4 Ensure that each magic word (what, why, when, how, where and who) is used only once.
5 The children are allowed only six questions.
6 The challenge is to get the maximum amount of information with the six questions.
7 Each learning pair now joins another pair and questions them using the same rules.
8 At the end of the activity, the pairs give feedback to the larger group and share what the challenges were.
9 Summarize the learning points.
10 Conclude.

Tip

Talk about the six magic words and how helpful they are to obtain comprehensive information. Close-ended questions are answered with 'yes' or 'no' and the information they supply is therefore limited. Open-ended questions provide answers that are fuller and more flexible.

Timing

5 minutes introduction and brief

15 minutes role play

10 minutes feedback and discussion

2 minutes concluding

6 Questions

I keep six honest serving men, they taught me all I know: their names are What and Why and When and How and Where and Who.

Rudyard Kipling

Six magic words

🛇🛇 Share in pairs

Each person in the learning pair thinks of an enjoyable experience. Don't say anything to your partner. Your challenge is to find out as much as possible about your partner's experience by asking the right questions.

When you are being questioned, only offer the information that is specifically asked for. Do not keep on talking unless it is the answer to a question.

Game rules

You must ask six questions only using the question words What? Why? When? How? Where? and Who?.

You may not use the question words more than once.

At the end of the activity, you and your partner must decide whether you have managed to get all the important information about each other's story by using the six words.

Tip!

You really have to plan your questions well if you are only allowed to use each word once! Try thinking of your questions before you start using the words at the top.

Small group

Try joining up with another pair and take turns to question them in order to test your progress.

Guidelines: Activity Sheet 7

Listening skills

Learning points

A good listener displays certain behaviours such as leaning forward, keeping eye contact, listening without interrupting, asking relevant questions, etc. These skills can be learnt!

Comments

1 Instruct the children to organise themselves in groups of three and sit down.
2 The children decide who are person 'A', 'B' and 'C' in each group.
3 *Round one.*
   a) Take persons 'A' out of the room. Tell them that they are going to be story-tellers and instruct them to prepare to tell the group about their best holiday or their hobbies. They will have to talk for about 2 minutes to be sure to finish their stories. While they prepare outside, go inside and instruct 'B' to be an observer and 'C' to be a listener. They have to really listen to the story-teller for the first 40 seconds and when you give a secret sign, such as coughing or taking a sip of water, they must then pretend to lose interest.
   b) Bring back the storytellers and instruct them to sit with their groups. Everybody has to be seated before you give them permission to commence the activity.
   c) After 40 seconds of story-telling, give the secret sign. Listeners and observers have to lose interest in a way that is clear to see. This feels very rude, but the experience is important. After about 1 minute of non-attentive listening, stop the game.
   d) Ask the story-tellers what they have experienced – normally they will be amazed by the rudeness. After listening to them, explain what has happened.
   e) Ask the listener how it felt to be rude.
   f) Ask the observer for feedback.
4 *Round two*
   This time brief persons 'B' outside the room. Give them the same instructions as the others before them. While persons 'B' prepare their stories, instruct the listeners in the room to interrupt when the secret sign is given. All roles are rotated, so there will be a different listener and observer each time. Choose a different secret sign this time, and allow 40 to 60 seconds before giving the sign.
5 *Round three*
   Take out persons 'C'. They get the same instructions as before. Repeat the game, only this time listener 'B' and observer 'A' listen with the utmost dedication and show real interest. The story-teller will probably wait for the secret sign, but nothing happens. Allow the listening to continue for about one and a half minutes and then stop the game and ask for feedback.

6 Now list on the board everything that can be observed when watching an empathic listener. For example: make eye contact, lean forward, ask relevant questions, have the right facial expression, say 'Hm, uh-uh', etc. to indicate that you are listening, invite the person to tell you more, etc.

Tip

This activity is an experiential exercise with the emphasis on how it feels when another pays proper attention. The opposite is also true: poor listeners make others feel disappointed and bad about themselves.

Timing

2 minutes instruction time for each group (persons A, B and C respectively) (6 minutes in total)

1 minute (×3) for settling down when groups return to the room and getting ready for the role play

2 minutes for the role play (×3)

2 minutes for asking the storytellers how they experienced the situation, and for observers to share what they have noticed (×3)

3 minutes to de-role and summarize learning points

7 Listening skills

👥👥👥 Small group of 3

Think about the best holiday you ever had, or a hobby you really enjoy. You are each going to take turns talking to the others in the group about your experiences.

Decide within the group, who are going to be persons 'A', 'B' and 'C' for the duration of the activity.

Exercise 1	Exercise 2	Exercise 3
A – speaker	A – listener	A – observer
B – observer	B – speaker	B – listener
C – listener	C – observer	C – speaker

At this stage, your teacher will explain to you how to perform the activity.

Remember, only start talking to the others once you have been given permission to do so by your teacher. All the groups will start their conversations at exactly the same time.

At the end of the activity, share your experiences within your group. Use the box below to list all the behaviours of a wonderful listener.

Use your list to give feedback to the larger group.

A good listener ...

Guidelines: Activity Sheet 8

I don't like it when another person...

Learning points

Listening skills are trainable. When you know what irritates you, you probably know what to work on. Quite often what irritates you most about others are things that you also do.

Comments

1 Instruct the children to read through the list on Activity Sheet 8 and to tick the behaviours that bother them.
2 Be prepared to assist where necessary.
3 This activity 'sets the scene' and serves as preparation for Activity 9.

Timing

3 minutes giving instructions

5–10 minutes self-assessment depending on the children's work speed

Feedback will be more appropriate after Activity 9.

8 I don't like it when another person...

👤 On your own

Read through the list below and tick the behaviours you do not like.

I hate it when another person...

1 interrupts me. ☐
2 pretends to listen – but does not hear what I say. ☐
3 only talks about himself. ☐
4 asks too many questions. ☐
5 talks about things I am not interested in. ☐
6 tells me what to do. ☐
7 answers a mobile phone while we talk. ☐
8 always tells me her story when I am trying to tell her mine. ☐
9 does not look into my eyes. ☐
10 gives solutions to my problems before he even understands. ☐

How many ticks have you made?

Guidelines: Activity Sheet 9

Uh...mmm!

Learning points

What irritates us about others is often true for ourselves.

Comments

1 Instruct the children to tick the items they find themselves doing.
2 After the self-assessment, discuss what they have learnt.
3 Conclude with general remarks, and point out that behaviours we dislike the most in other people are often the same as those we display.

Timing

2 minutes instructions

5–10 minutes self-assessment

10 minutes learning points, summarizing, conclusion

9 Uh…mmm!

👤 On your own

Read through the list below and tick the behaviours that are sometimes true for you.

If I were honest with myself, I sometimes…

1 interrupt others. ☐
2 pretend to listen – but do not really hear what the other person says. ☐
3 talk only about myself. ☐
4 ask too many questions. ☐
5 talk about things the other person is not interested in. ☐
6 tell others what they should do. ☐
7 answer my mobile phone while we are talking. ☐
8 tell my story when they are trying to tell me theirs. ☐
9 do not look into their eyes. ☐
10 give solutions to their problems before I even understand. ☐

1   How many ticks have you made this time?

2   What have you learnt from doing this activity?
    Write your answer in the box below.

Guidelines: Activity Sheet 10

Listening for feelings

Learning points

Listening for feelings is not about making assumptions, giving advice, criticism or instructions. It is about hearing the emotions behind the words and checking for your understanding. In essence it is about acknowledging the other person's reality.

Comments

1 Explain the principle of empathic listening.
2 Read the phrases one by one and each time instruct a child or learning pair to write their response in the space provided on the right-hand side.
3 Your voice tone is important. You could try saying the same phrase more than once changing the voice tone each time. This allows for more participation and helps to clarify the role of non-verbal communication in the interpretation of emotions.
4 Read the phrases for a second time and for every phrase ask the responsible child or learning pair to read out their written answers to the instructions given in 2 above. Encourage wider participation by inviting other children or pairs to verbally share their interpretations of the same phrases, based on your voice tone. Discuss the probability that people understand words and voice tones differently and that more than one response can be appropriate.

This activity demonstrates how empathic listening is about ensuring that you understand the other person's reality from their point of view. It is *not* about judging or imposing your ideas, opinions or interpretations upon the other person. In essence, the response of the empathic listener is a reflection or mirror of the *emotions* of the other person.

What empathic listening is *not*:

Giving advice: 'You should …' or 'What you should do, is…'

Blaming: 'It is because you have…'

Probing: 'Why?' 'How can you say that?'

Imposing your ideas: 'Let me tell you how it really works…'

Tip

Make sure to clarify the principle that empathic listening is about trying to understand the other person's reality and not about judging it according to an individual's frame of reference or preference. Use humour.

Timing

5 minutes introduction

25 minutes participation

5 minutes concluding

Examples

These are only a few options, there could be many more:

The other person says:	You respond:
0 *You always hurt me.*	*You feel injured/heartbroken/sad.*
1 You don't listen to me.	So, you feel ignored/unimportant/unloved?
2 You are a bully.	You feel hurt/done in?
3 I wish it were mine.	You feel envious/cheated/sad/longing?
4 I can never tell you how I feel.	You feel ignored/underestimated/misunderstood?
5 I cannot stand you!	You feel frustrated/hurt/angry/resentful/irritated?
6 I just want to leave this place.	So you feel overwhelmed/overburdened/scared?
7 They always forget about me.	You feel disappointed/discouraged/ignored?
8 It is such a big job!	You feel scared/tired/overwhelmed?
9 Do you think I look good enough?	You are unsure/uncertain/doubtful of yourself?
10 I know that I failed the test.	You feel negative/disappointed/discouraged?

10 Listening for feelings

Do you know how to listen for feelings? Try and change the comments under 'The other person says' to a proper response that reflects the feelings of the other person. Use example 0 as a guide. Then write your answers in the space under the heading 'You respond' and be prepared to share your responses with the group when it is your turn. This activity helps you to name the feelings that the other person is experiencing.

The other person says:	**You respond:**
0 *You always hurt me.*	*You feel injured/heartbroken/sad?*
1 You don't listen to me.	
2 You are a bully.	
3 I wish it were mine.	
4 I can never tell you how I feel.	
5 I cannot stand you!	
6 I just want to leave this place.	
7 They always forget about me.	
8 It is such a big job!	
9 Do you think I look good enough?	
10 I know that I failed the test.	

Reflection

How does it make people feel when you truly listen to them?

Satisfied

Happy

Surprised

Tired

Concentrating

Disapproving

Pained

Obstinate

Shocked

Undecided

Puzzled

Mischievous

Guidelines: Activity Sheet 11

Empathic listening

Learning points

Empathic listening is a skill needed by everybody. It is particularly useful when helping others deal with upsetting emotions.

Comments

1 Children work in pairs for this activity. Each pair has one sentence to formulate. If there are more than 20 participants, some pairs will have the same question. Assign a question to each pair.

2 Each child in the pair takes a turn at answering the allocated question. The pair then formulate one appropriate response on behalf of the pair. There are no right answers, but ensure that answers are not advising, criticizing or instructing.

3 Once every pair has completed the response, the pairs take turns to share their answer with the large group. For each answer, make suggestions if necessary. In the case of a good response, acknowledge the success and point out what made it good.

4 Give acknowledgement and guidance, but do not expect complete understanding, as this is an advanced skill.

5 Remember, the answers below are only possibilities. There could be many more. Keep in mind that the activity is about reflecting the other person's emotions.

Timing

10 minutes introduction and explanation

25+ minutes preparing and sharing individual responses in the larger group

5 minutes concluding

Note

Activity 11 is a more advanced version of Activity 10, which is a simpler form of active listening and works as a scaffolding activity, helping children to first master the identification of emotions or feelings, based on the phrases and the voice tone of the teacher reading them out.

Activity 11 goes further in that it requires the formulation of a whole sentence and is therefore addressing not only the emotion, but also the context in which the emotion is/was expressed.

Examples

0 Teacher says that the marks are final.
Learner says: 'I want higher marks. My answer was correct!'
Teacher responds: 'You feel frustrated when I don't want to change your marks?'

1 Mother says the room is not neat enough.
Child says: 'Now I have to tidy my room again. You never tell me beforehand what you want me to do about my room!'
Mother responds: 'So you feel angry that I haven't explained what I want you to do clearly enough?' Or 'You feel frustrated when I don't give you clear guidelines?'

2 Child has to finish his chores before the weekend.
Father says: 'You never finish your chores on time.'
Child responds: 'So you feel disappointed when I don't do what you expect from me?' Or 'So you feel uncertain that I will do what I am supposed to do?'

3 Father is not trying out the child's suggestions.
Child says: 'Why don't you ever listen to me?'
Father responds: 'So you feel frustrated when I don't try your ideas?' Or 'So you feel disappointed when you offer suggestions and I don't take notice?'

4 Family is not on time for school.
Mother says: 'I get tired of waiting for children every morning!'
Child responds: 'You are irritated when we don't do things on time/don't prepare beforehand/are disorganized?'

5 Teacher gives out a group assignment.
Child says: 'I don't want to work with Joe on any more assignments. He never finishes on time!'
Teacher responds: 'So you don't want to work with others who are not punctual?'

6 Child has not handed in the last homework.
Teacher says: 'Can't you be as dedicated as the rest of the group and hand your homework in on time?'
Learner responds: 'You feel frustrated when my work is not handed in on time/when I fail to hand my work in on the set date?'

7 Sports coach has started a different training programme.
Player says: 'We tried something like this three years ago and it didn't work then.'
Coach responds: 'So you are frustrated when we use programmes that we have used before/when we revert to old programmes/when we change our training methods?'

8 Child representative notices that another child is talking so loud that others cannot concentrate.
Representative says: 'Can't you be more considerate while others are trying to work?'
Child responds: 'So you feel frustrated when I am disturbing others/when I talk loud while others work?'

9 Teacher decides to change the curriculum of a subject.
Child says: 'You give us too much extra work. I can never get it all done.'
Teacher responds: 'You feel frustrated when I improvise/give you unscheduled work/make changes to the work plan?'

10 Child has refused to do homework over the weekend.
Teacher says: 'Young people of today are lazy.'
Student responds: 'So you feel disappointed when we don't want to put in extra effort/do not do what is expected of us?'

11 Empathic listening

👥 Share in pairs

This activity is very similar to Activity 10, but goes a little further. During this activity, you do not only describe the feelings of the other person, but you also name the reason for the person's feelings. Work with your learning partner and write down your response to the comment from below that your teacher has allocated to you. Each pair will get the opportunity to prepare and deliver a response.

Once everybody has a response, you will each read your response out loud to the large group when it is your turn.

You can decide who will read out the response to the group. Make sure that you take turns to speak on behalf of the pair or group.

You may learn from the other pairs, and they could make comments on your response.

There are, of course, many ways of responding, but the important thing is to reflect or mirror the other person's emotions. You do not answer or give your opinion or solutions, but simply repeat the other person's emotion in your own words.

You base your response more on the voice tone and body language than the person's actual words.

Example:

Teacher says that the marks are final.

Learner says: 'I want higher marks. My answer was correct!'

Teacher responds: 'You feel frustrated when I don't want to change your marks?'

---

1   Mother says the room is not neat enough.

Child says: 'Now I have to tidy my room again. You never tell me beforehand what you want me to do about my room!'

Mother responds:

2   Child has to finish his chores before the weekend.

Father says: 'You never finish your chores on time.'

Child responds:

3   Father is not trying out the child's suggestions.

Child says: 'Why don't you ever listen to me?'

Father responds:

4   Family is not on time for school.

Mother says: 'I get tired of waiting for children every morning!'

Child responds:

11 *Empathic listening* (continued)

5   Teacher gives out a group assignment.

Child says: 'I don't want to work with Joe on any more assignments. He never finishes on time!'

Teacher responds:

6   Child has not handed in the last homework.

Teacher says: 'Can't you be as dedicated as the rest of the group and hand your homework in on time?'

Learner responds:

7   Sports coach has started a different training programme.

Player says: 'We tried something like this three years ago and it didn't work then.'

Coach responds:

8   Child representative notices that another child is talking so loud that others cannot concentrate.

Representative says: 'Can't you be more considerate while others are trying to work?'

Child responds:

9   Teacher decides to change the curriculum of a subject.

Child says: 'You give us too much extra work. I can never get it all done.'

Teacher responds:

10   Child has refused to do homework over the weekend.

Teacher says: 'Young people of today are lazy.'

Student responds:

12 *Action plan*

My name is:

👥 Small group

Work in a group of 4 or 5 and write down ten things people notice about an empathic person.

1

2

3

4

5

6

7

8

9

10

For the next part of the activity, you need to pass your activity sheet to each person in your group and ask them to tick one thing/item on the list that you can change to help make you more empathic.

Each of you, on your own, write down three things you would like to work on in order to be more empathic.

1

2

3

Finding solutions

I can

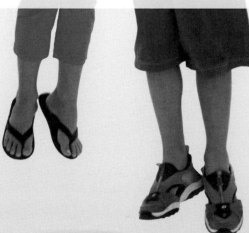

Outline

Outcomes

On completion of this unit, children should have the knowledge, skills and attitudes to deal with problems effectively. To be able to solve problems they will need to:

- know that they choose how they feel and respond.
- believe that they can solve their problems.
- understand that different problems need to be solved in different ways.
- follow certain steps to solve problems.
- think with reason and be creative.
- create different ideas to choose from.
- work through personal problems.
- know where to look for help.
- ask for help when it is needed.
- help others where they can.
- say 'no' when someone asks them to do something unreasonable.

The distress that a person may feel is not a result of what actually exists objectively. It is a result of how the person perceives what is happening.

Al Siebert (1996)

Overview

Are children natural survivors?

We are all born with natural resilience. A baby falls while learning to walk and, within minutes, the child is ready to try again.

Herbert S. Kindler (1993)

It is said that children of today are more intelligent than their parents. Some researchers even suggest that their IQ is higher. But emotional problems still seem to be a big challenge according to the findings of authors such as Stephen Covey, Daniel Goleman and others.

Problem solving requires logical as well as creative and emotional inputs, depending on the type of problem. Many useful models teach thinking skills and practical problem-solving strategies, but most people (especially children) find emotional problems taxing. For such problems you need to combine reasoning with emotional processing. This workbook offers guidelines for dealing with personal and interpersonal problems with emotional implications. It covers strategies for knowing what to do when you do not know what to do.

Nobody is invincible!

In the past, people who functioned well despite adversity were described as being invincible or invulnerable. This is an over simplification. Although some individuals may be more resistant than others, everyone has limitations. When you stretch yourself beyond your limits, you may perceive the experience as exhilarating. However, when you consider the long-term side-effects, you would be wise to take the occasional break before you break!

Resilience is not an unchanging characteristic. Despite being vulnerable at times, you can overcome problems and progress to live a successful, happy life. Just as the current factors in your life that work do not ensure future successes, the mishaps also do not need to hamper you forever. To grow into a strong, hardy individual, you need to deal with challenges.

When you learn to apply the right strategies, challenges turn into valuable experiences.

Don't let problems kill you!

You could be winning and feel like you are losing because your scorecard is unfair.

Emotional problems can be very complex. You do not always understand why you react the way you do, and working it out could take time, but you can choose how you deal with challenges. This is based on your inner talk or 'inner working models', which refer to your personal beliefs and basic outlook on life. Although such beliefs are strong and normally long standing, you need to consciously modify or change them when you gain new insight or wisdom.

Choosing outcomes

Your distress is not always a logical result of what is actually happening – your personal experience is based on your subjective perception of the situation. The table on page 47 shows how our conscious choices can influence our experience of events.

Some people deal with problems in a very serious, aggressive, task-oriented and time-conscious way, driving themselves and others hard to get results. In her book *Focus of Mind and Body* (1997), Linda Wasmer Smith refers to work done by Meyer Friedman and Ray Rosenman in which they explain that so-called Personality Type A behaviours could lead to coronary disease. However, later studies indicated that the same task-driven attributes corresponded with a speedy recovery (faster than others) from illness because of dedication and discipline in following doctor's orders!

Personality Type B individuals are described as 'the nicest people' (because of their friendliness and accommodating nature), and handle problems in a different way. They are 'people-pleasers' and are therefore affected by others and their issues. In fact, psychologists Temoshok and Dreher (1992) went further and created a third category of stress

Positive choices		Negative choices	
Process	**Result**	**Process**	**Result**
Courage ↓	Confidence	Apathy ↓	Withdrawal
Cope ↓	Internal locus of control	Intimidation ↓	External locus of control
Trust ↓	Respect	Mistrust ↓	Anxious
Visualize ↓	Direction	Despair ↓	Depression
Hope ↓	Optimism	Aggression ↓	Maladjusted
Believe ↓	Responsibility	Fear ↓	No hope
Adapt ↓	Adjustment	Blame ↓	Victim
Renew ↓	Flexibility	Resignation ↓	Resentment
Succeed ↓	Healthy self-esteem	Fail ↓	Poor self-esteem
Joy and happiness		**Unhappiness and resentment**	

behaviours linked to a Type C (for cancer) behaviour pattern. Typical behaviours include:

- doing things for others, instead of attending to personal issues.
- bottling up unpleasant emotions instead of expressing them.
- putting up with other people's demands instead of standing up for their rights.

These categories of behaviours do not offer the full answer. It may be reasonable to assume that how you deal with problems is entirely unique to you as a person. Yet, when investigating factors that influence resilience, it is helpful to learn from those who recovered from trauma or significant set-backs to live productive, happy lives. Optimism is a typical trait of highly resilient individuals. Psychologist Martin

Seligman's (1990) well-known work on optimism and healing supports the optimism theory. He maintained that your so-called explanatory style ('inner talk' – the way in which you routinely explain to yourself why things happen) is crucial to your health. When you deal with problems you either feel energized or helpless. If you tend to believe that causes of bad events are permanent and out of your control, you start to feel like a victim and display 'learned helplessness' because you believe you are helpless, when in fact you could do something about your circumstances.

So, apart from positive thinking, what else can help you deal with problems effectively? Jeff Levin (quoted in Wasmer Smith, 1997), an associate professor of family health and community medicine at Eastern

Virginia Medical School, reported on scores of studies that link practising religion with health. He concluded that religion possibly helps people cope with problems because religious traditions:

- create a sense of belonging
- address belief systems promoting peace, confidence and meaning
- include religious rites and rituals which may relieve stress
- promote faith and hope that leads to healing
- support wholesome habits
- are about love, the most fundamental issue of all.

The opposite is also true. Some studies suggest that by watching violent television programmes (which of course shows scenes of how people handle problems in the worst possible way) you could harm your health. Your body experiences the symptoms of fear, anger and hatred generated on screen, especially if the person being harmed is of the same gender as you. So, by keeping your mind busy with negativity, you create problems for yourself.

All this proves that emotions have a major impact on how you cope with problems and the effect they have on you. The good news is that emotions can be managed. You can train yourself to be positive by managing your thoughts and beliefs. If emotions are the result of events, filtered through beliefs, then changing your beliefs changes the nature of problems because problems are not the actual events themselves, but rather how we feel about the events. Change your belief system and you change your problems. Health is therefore a choice.

Count your words!

Your thinking patterns are reflected in your choice of words. Words represent images or metaphors. By listening to the words a person uses, you can get an idea of how that person views life. Conversely, word choices have a profound influence on how you experience events. So, it is a twofold process of addressing beliefs and word choices. It works both ways.

[I]t is through language that we create the world, because it's nothing until we describe it. And when we describe it, we create distinctions that govern our actions. To put it another way, we do not describe the world we see, but we see the world we describe.

Joseph Jawarski (quoted by Sue Knight, 1995)

Therefore, what we describe internally becomes our reality externally.

Sue Knight (1995) explains how certain phrases represent specific metaphors, which in turn create unique company cultures. You can make fairly accurate assumptions about the culture of a company by observing the words and actions of employees. Culture is an expression of the values promoted and rewarded within the company and represents the general outlook in the specific company. If that is the case, what type of culture could you expect in the two examples below? Notice the difference in emotional reaction when you compare the following two categories of metaphors:

Being in the firing line.	Everything looks rosy.
Attacking the competition.	The company is blooming.
Aiming at the target.	Business has died down.
Combating his response.	There is organic growth.

Ask yourself:

- Which set of metaphors do you prefer?
- How would each metaphor influence your approach to problems?
- Think about your school: what is the metaphor in your school?
- Which words come up regularly in discussions?
- How do you talk to and about children?
- What would be an acceptable metaphor for you personally?

Despite actively creating a positive reality through the use of words, you are bombarded with negativity in the media. But, Paramahansa Yogananda (1994) said:

Evil spreads with the wind. Truth is able to travel against the wind.

Therefore, positive thoughts and actions can override the negative influences in your surroundings.

Common sense

Being positive does not mean that you see only the bright side of events. It simply means that you also see the bright side. Optimism refers more to hope than to unrealistic or selective thinking. Being optimistic includes the acknowledgement of obstacles and possible threats or problems, while balancing them with a bright outlook and problem-solving attitude as opposed to feeling at the mercy, and becoming the victim, of events.

Exceptionally resilient people sometimes feel like misfits, seldom understood by others. They are expected to always be strong and not have to ask others for emotional help or support. They are so hardy and persistent they may not give up when they should. When they counterbalance optimistic thinking by anticipating what might go wrong, they can be mistakenly labelled by a group as a negative person.

Al Siebert (1996)

Recovering from setbacks

No road is without bumps, potholes and side-tracking events. You can either call these obstacles problems or you can think of them as challenges. How you deal with challenges determines what you get out of life.

The ultimate measure of a man is not where he stands in moments of comfort, but where he stands at times of challenge and discovery.

Martin Luther King Jr.

However, you are born with an amazing gift to overcome adversity – to bounce back and heal from hurt and disappointment. Just think of the many stories of true survivors, their recovery and outstanding achievements.

Response able, account able and act knowledge

The more control a person feels over a situation, the more responsibility he will exhibit.

Kurt Hanks (1991)

To be responsible in this context means that you are willing and able to respond. You have a choice in terms of how you handle situations. Although you might not be able to control what happens to you, or understand why it is happening to you, you have a choice in terms of how you respond – you are: Response Able.

The term 'accountability' stems from an ancient Roman term, which means 'to stand forth and be "counted"'. The idea of 'accountability' acknowledges that you created, promoted or allowed what happened in your life. This is the opposite of being at the mercy of others or circumstance. When you accept accountability, you reclaim your personal power.

When you acknowledge something you admit that you are aware of the situation. You 'act knowingly'. You may not consciously contribute to making something happen, but it is possible that you may play a part in it. It is not blame, faultfinding, reproach, criticism or the burden of guilt. It is a simple statement of presence and ownership.

Creativity and quiet time

It is a healthy personal strategy to set aside time for quiet contemplation. Many of the great discoveries in history were made during times of loneliness or isolation. While talking to others can be helpful or healing and brainstorming works well for solving problems in group context, the creativity needed for personal renewal has different requirements.

During walks in nature, journal writing, meditation and reflection, you get in touch with yourself and your personal beliefs and values. With that connection secured, decision making is more aligned with your personal needs.

Humour

Eric Hoffer, an American sociologist, stated: 'The compulsion to take ourselves seriously is in inverse proportion to our creative capacity.'

The message is clear: don't take yourself and your challenges too seriously. Laughter has turned more than one stressful situation into a creative opportunity. Laughter lightens up problematic issues and promotes good health. I am convinced that a well-organized, hardworking, service-oriented organisation in which there is also humour and laughter is 'nicer' (more enjoyable) to work in, and is therefore a healthier company with possibly less absenteeism. Laughter heals! At the least, it soothes pain – physical and otherwise.

> I made the joyous discovery that ten minutes of genuine belly laughter had an anesthetic effect and would give me at least two hours of pain-free sleep.
>
> *Norman Cousins (quoted in Wasmer Smith 1997)*

More remedies for problems could be:

- chatting to friends
- keeping pets
- playing or listening to music
- practising or appreciating art
- helping others.

When you help others, it helps you to see your own problems in perspective.

Acceptance

Solving problems is an attitude – a solution-oriented outlook on life. Most problems can be solved with conscious effort. Some, however, are beyond your control, and then acceptance is the wisest option. To keep on fighting and debating things you cannot change, simply deplete your personal resources and can alienate you from others.

> Lord, give me the courage
> to change the things which can and ought
> to be changed,
> the serenity
> to accept the things which cannot be changed,
> and the wisdom
> to know the difference.
>
> *Alcoholics Anonymous Prayer*

Guidelines
and
Activity Sheets

Guidelines: Activity Sheet 1

Thinking, dreaming, scheming

Learning points

Working on problems may include structured thinking, following specific steps. However, many problems are solved in a way that can be difficult to explain through logic. This is what is known as gut feel – a combination of experience and intuition. Some people refer to an inner guidance. Some will say that God gave them the answers. Whichever way you prefer to phrase it, the message is that it sometimes helps to hold lightly onto problems, even letting go of them, instead of forcefully working on them, to eventually produce the best end results. Sometimes you make things worse when you constantly focus on the solution of a problem. It obstructs your thinking.

Comments

1 Ask the children whether they have ever found a brilliant idea for something, when they were busy with something totally unrelated, such as sitting in the bath or taking a shower.
2 Ask them to complete the self-assessment questionnaire and share it with a learning partner.
3 Ask for inputs from the larger group.
4 Conclude by saying that creative thoughts are more likely to occur when you are relaxed.

Timing

2 minutes introduction

4 minutes self-assessment

4 minutes discussion

2 minutes general discussion and concluding

1 *Thinking, dreaming, scheming*

👥 Share in pairs

Complete the self-assessment questionnaire below by putting a tick in the boxes that apply to you. When you have finished, share your answers with a learning partner.

Self-assessment questionnaire

1   Have you ever wanted something, got it, and found out you wanted something else? ☐

2   Do you sometimes have a plan, and while you are working on the plan, you find a better one? ☐

3   Are there times when you are glad that you did not know about something? ☐

4   Do you sometimes dream about things and just do wishful thinking? ☐

5   Is it sometimes impossible to explain why you have made a certain decision? ☐

6   Is it a good idea that you sometimes decide not to decide? ☐

7   Have you ever known beforehand what was going to happen? ☐

Understanding your results

If you said 'yes' to some of the questions, it means that you do not always make decisions in a way that is easy to explain to others. Sometimes you make the best decisions when you just follow your heart. Some people talk about 'gut feel' or 'intuition'.

You are supposed to use your head and your heart. It means at times you have to follow rules and at other times you need to find new ways of doing things.

Points to remember

When facing any problem you need to remember that you are:

● Responsible – you are able to respond. You can choose how you feel about something, and what you are going to do about it.

● Accountable – you need to able to live with the results or consequences of what you do.

● Free to choose – blaming others or postponing action will not get you where you want to be.

Guidelines: Activity Sheet 2

Logical thinking

Learning points

Most people feel more secure with reasoning, because it does not involve high levels of emotional involvement and empathy. However, it is important to realise that when a practical or mathematical problem, such as the ones offered in this activity, is difficult for you, you should not take it personally and turn it into an emotional issue. For instance, if you believe you should be able to do something but you do not manage it, your belief system becomes the obstacle. While you may have other talents, you could think less of yourself because of this particular 'lack of talent'. A very successful maths teacher repeatedly stated that the psychology of maths is a crucial factor in achievement – take away the stress around the subject, build self-esteem, make the learning fun and the marks improve.

Comments

1 This is a short, fun-filled activity.
2 Keep pages face down, until the children are instructed to start. First explain what is expected, then say: 'You can turn your pages now. Start!'
3 First activity: fill in the missing number.
4 Second activity: move only three boxes.
5 Third activity: count the number of squares.
6 The children are to work on their own, or share with learning partners as pairs, small groups, large groups, or girls versus boys. They decide what works for them.
7 You could make this a competition and challenge the children to solve it as quickly as possible.
8 At the end, ask them to reflect on how it felt to solve the practical problems, and how it is different from solving emotional problems.

Answer to first activity: 4, or 40, depending on whether you started with 4 or ended there. (The pattern is + 2 + 3 + 4 etc.)

Answer to second activity:

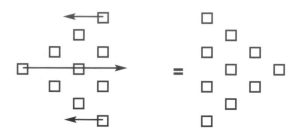

Answer to third activity: 30 squares. Logic behind it:

One large (complete diagram) =**1**

16 small = **16** in total

Units of 2 × 2 squares each: 4 quadrants + 1 in the middle, + 4 in the middle left, right, top and bottom = **9** in total

Units of 3 × 3 = **4** in total

Grand total = **30**

However, there is no right or wrong answer! This is a perceptual exercise, answers such as '1' or '16' or '4' should not be viewed as wrong, but rather ask: 'How did you look at it?' 'What did you see?' The rationale is that reality is what each person sees or notices as an individual, and we should take that into account when solving problems.

Timing

2 minutes introduction and outlining the activity

5 minutes completing the activity

2 minutes concluding

2 Logical thinking

👥👥 Small group activity

1 Which number is the missing one in the diagram?

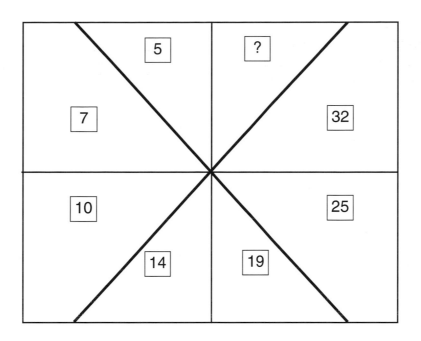

2 Move only three boxes to reverse the arrangement. (So the new arrangement has four boxes on the left tapering to one box on the right.)

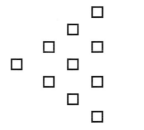

3 How many squares in the diagram?

Guidelines: Activity Sheet 3

Creative thinking

Learning points

Answers are unlimited and even wacky. Creativity is about surprising ideas, not predictable ones.

Comments

1 Read through the questions and clarify uncertainties.
2 Instruct the children to work as small groups of five to ten. Too few or too many children make the activity either too low in energy and ideas, or tedious and less effective.
3 Talk about the experience of working with others and inspiring each other to come up with ideas.

Tip

Encourage creative, unusual thinking and respect for others' ideas, even though they might seem odd or unworkable at the time. Point out the principles of brainstorming, which includes piggybacking on others' ideas, no criticism, open-minded thinking and no evaluation during the brainstorming activity. Normally groups of 8–12 children work best for brainstorming, but in a large group the facilitator may have more control over the process. It is important that each child makes an input and that it is treated with respect.

Timing

2 minutes instructing

10 minutes practical work

3 minutes concluding

3 *Creative thinking*

👥 Small group activity

1 You have to take something to a friend's house. Your arms and hands are full. You need to take one more bag. How many ways can you think of to carry the extra bag?

2 Think of something you really like. Imagine putting it into a see-through plastic bag. Imagine this object or thing or idea fitting into the bag, even though it may be very large in real life. When you rub the bag between your hands, what happens inside the bag? When you open the bag, what does it smell like?

3 Find the best name for a dark brown dog that has only one ear and loves raisins.

Guidelines: Activity Sheet 4

Six-step problem solving model

Learning points

By following certain steps, you can address a wide range of problems.

Comments

1 Briefly go through the steps, explaining how the model works. Follow the instructions on the Activity Sheet 4.
2 The children solve the problem by applying the skills in small groups.
3 At the end of the process, small groups give feedback to the larger group.
4 Ask: 'Which part of the activity is easier?' 'What is more difficult?' 'How can you use the model?'

Tip

Tell the children that even large companies use the basic Six-step Problem Solving method regularly to address problems.

You may benefit from having one group demonstrate by role playing the whole process while you guide, make inputs and adjustments. For the role play you are welcome to come up with a different scenario, or allow the group to select the option they prefer. The groups then solve 'their problems' using the same principles. Small groups can choose one of the two options to work on.

Timing

5 minutes introduction

15 minutes role play

25 minutes small group activity

15 minutes feedback and concluding

4 *Six-step problem solving model*

♟♟♟ Small group activity

Option 1

Your school is planning a Fun Day. Your class is responsible for setting up a food stall to sell hamburgers. How are you going to make sure that your stall is successful? All class members are supposed to take part.

Option 2

As a group of friends, you plan to appear on a popular TV show. To qualify, you have to present something (singing, acting, a humorous act, gymnastics, etc.) for entertainment as part of the screening test. What now?

Step 1: What is the problem?

● What should be done?

● What is the task?

● What are some of the difficulties that you will have to overcome?

● What worries you about the task/problem?

4 Six-step problem solving model (continued)

Step 2: What do you want?

- What do you want, or what do think you want?
- Describe a 'picture' of what you want.
- What will make you say: This is great! This is good!

Step 3: How will you get the solution?

- What should be done to get the end result you want?
- Everybody comes up with ideas, and someone writes these down, without criticizing or judging.
- Build on each other's ideas. Add to the list.
- Remember when you offer ideas, the ideas become the 'property of the list', not of the person offering it. So, when an idea at first does not seem to be a good one, do not criticize or tease the person. Simply list the idea. This works best on a large sheet of paper or on a board that everybody can see.

4 Six-step problem solving model (continued)

Step 4: Select the best idea

- As a group, use the list of ideas that you wrote down in Step 3 and consider the ideas, one by one. Now is the time to decide what is possible and what can work.
- Tick the workable ideas and draw a line through the ideas that seem to be less workable.

Step 5: Draw up a plan

- How are you going to do it?
- Write down the steps for doing the task. (You may use a project planner for the purpose.)
- Decide who is going to do which part of the task.
- Give each task a date when it has to be completed.
- Appoint a responsible person to act as co-ordinator, manager or team leader. This person will make sure that everybody is doing what they should be doing to get the work done.

Tasks	Responsible person
1	
2	
3	
4	
5	

Step 6: Follow up

- The team leader should call the group together occasionally to ensure that everybody is clear on what they should be doing, and when it has to be done.
- If someone is not pulling their weight, the team leader will talk to the person on behalf of the team.
- If necessary, change the jobs of anyone who cannot handle what they should be doing. But, be careful – do not change too often. The group has to work together and help each other where possible.
- As a group, decide what is the biggest challenge during this phase of the project, if it was to happen in real life. Write your answer in the box below.

Guidelines: Activity Sheet 5

Finding solutions

Learning points

Problem solving involves analytical thinking – taking apart the elements of the situation and evaluating their effects on the situation. Identifying what is wrong is often the first step in effective problem solving. This could easily lead to blaming someone instead of clarifying responsibilities. This part of the problem-solving process could be tiring.

The second element of the activity is the creative part in which the outcomes and possible solutions are generated. This is normally the more energetic and motivating aspect of dealing with issues. The challenge is to know what you want. Too often it is easier to know what you do not want.

Comments

1 Read through the steps, and then instruct the children to work in groups of five to get to an answer.
2 Invite each group to give feedback to the larger group.
3 Ask about personal experiences. Which part of the activity is more challenging? Which part is more rewarding or enjoyable?
4 Ask the children: where and when can you apply this in your lives?
5 Conclude.

Tip

Read through the framework first, clarifying what the questions mean.

Timing

5 minutes orientation

15 minutes group work

5 minutes feedback

3 minutes concluding

5 Finding solutions

♟♟♟ Small group activity

Imagine that for the group project one person simply does not offer help or contribute at all. You find yourself doing more and more, putting in some extra time. The final date is very close and everybody is under pressure. It is really important that everybody pulls their weight.

Step 1: Facing facts

Answer the following questions:

1 What is wrong? What is the problem?

2 Why do you have this problem?

3 How does this problem limit you?

4 Whose fault is it?

5 Who is in control?

Step 2: Focus on the outcome

Answer the following questions:

1 What is the ideal situation? What do you really want?

2 What can you do to make it happen?

3 What are the first steps towards the solution?

4 Who can help you to make it happen?

5 How will you know that you have achieved your goal?

Think about your emotional experience during the two steps of this activity. What can you learn from doing this activity?

Guidelines: Activity Sheet 6

Results window

Learning points

The results window is a simple tool to help you determine what the implications of decisions are for the individual as well as the group. It serves as a reality check and encourages children to consider the implications of their decisions. This is also a way of promoting empathy and social responsibility.

Comments

1 Read through the activity first, explaining what the purpose is.
2 Allow groups to work out the details in each window.
3 Groups report back on each window's outcomes.
4 Discuss their inputs.
5 Summarize.

Example

If, for instance, you keep on doing the work for the person who is not pulling his or her weight, this will be the result:

Tip

Point out to the children that everything we do could potentially impact on others.

Timing

5 minutes introduction

15 minutes group work

10 sharing and concluding

	Positive	Negative
Self	I feel good because I help the group progress. I gain experience.	I get overloaded. My own work does not get done. Others get irritated with me. I feel like a victim. I resent the negligent person.
Others	The work gets done. Others don't get extra work because I do it.	Because of my overload, they find my work is not done properly. There is no real team spirit. The project becomes a burden to everyone.

6 Results window

👥 Small group activity

You have made a decision during Activity 5. Use the following table to determine what the results or effects would be:

- Situation 1: You keep on allowing the person not to pull his or her weight (write this in blue).

- Situation 2: You address the problem and distribute work equally (write this in another colour, using the same table).

	Positive	Negative
Self		
Others		

👥 Large group discussion

- What do you notice about the number of items in each window?

- What is your conclusion about the two situations and the results one can expect in each case?

Guidelines: Activity Sheet 7

Planning a group project

Learning points

Clear guidelines prevent confusion, unnecessary stress and disagreement when team members have their own interpretation of what they should do. This guideline helps to structure the process of working together, clarifies tasks and responsibilities, and gives time frames.

Timing

5 minutes introduction

20 minutes application

5 minutes feedback

Comments

1 Instruct small groups to use the examples previously given in the Six-step Problem Solving Model.
2 The children complete the form, pretending to plan for the event, considering realistic time frames and breaking tasks into steps.
3 Ask: 'What have you learnt from doing this activity?'

Tip

Ask the group how they think a large project like the construction of a road or building is organized to be finished on time. 'Planning a group project' may be a bit simplistic for managing big projects like the construction of a building or road. For project management, other models are generally incorporated into the planning process. However, this activity is useful for structuring thoughts and tasks, and can be used in combination with other models.

The activity clarifies the complexity of time frames and job allocation in a simplified manner.

7 Planning a group project

👥👥 Small group activity

When you work on a group assignment it is important that each member of the group does their share of the work in time. The following table will help you organize your group and each person's part of the job, as well as the resources you will need.

Name of project:				
Tasks	**Resources needed**	**Action steps**	**Deadline**	**Responsible person**
1		1 2 3 4 5		
2		1 2 3 4 5		
3		1 2 3 4 5		
4		1 2 3 4 5		
5		1 2 3 4 5		

Guidelines: Activity Sheet 8

Solving personal problems model

Learning points

Personal problems are often so upsetting that you struggle not to revert to survival mode: fight (aggression), flight (avoid), freeze (get stuck), flock (group) or perhaps even to simply give up. By following a structured thinking process, you could help yourself and find out what to do when you do not know what to do.

Comments

1 Individuals go through the model, applying it to a problem and coming up with their own solutions.
2 Discuss the similarities and differences between the outcomes of different groups; and refer to the uniqueness of each person's situation and personality. Individuals need to decide what is right for them and it may be different from how another person prefers things to be. Children need to remember not to harm others, and to stay sensitive to the emotions of others as well.

Tip

Read through the model in the form of a brief overview. As a second round, ask for inputs as you go through each point.

Timing

5 minutes introduction

12 minutes individual work

10 minutes sharing, concluding

8 *Solving personal problems model*

👤 On your own

Think about something that has been bothering you for some time. You need to make a decision. If you cannot think of something that you personally need to deal with, think of someone else's dilemma and solve it 'on behalf' of the person. Here is an easy method to follow.

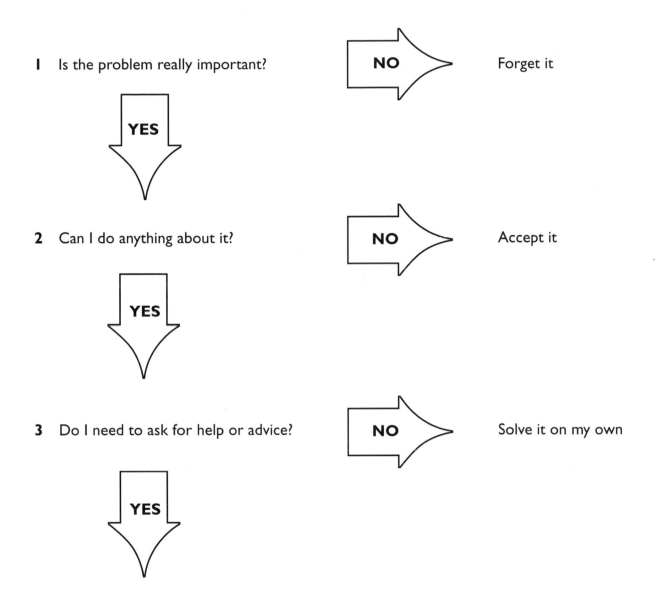

1   Is the problem really important? **NO** ⟶ Forget it

YES ↓

2   Can I do anything about it? **NO** ⟶ Accept it

YES ↓

3   Do I need to ask for help or advice? **NO** ⟶ Solve it on my own

YES ↓

**3   This is my problem, I will find help and solve it.
I will not give up!**

Guidelines: Activity Sheet 9

Solving personal problems

Learning points

Following a recipe can help you in times of emotional upheaval when you may become indecisive or too forced in your approach. In the case of bullying, a child will need the assistance of older people, and the school could reward good behaviour.

Comments

1 Talk through the steps first, answering questions and clarifying uncertainties.
2 Allow for individual work.
3 Feedback to the larger group, with learning points highlighted.

Tip

The children have written about a close friend or a bully who may be in the same class, so keep individual children's work confidential and just discuss broad themes when giving feedback to the larger group. Some children may have good advice to offer, based on their success strategies when dealing with a similar situation. This could be shared tactfully to help children learn from each other, without mentioning names or embarrassing others.

Timing

3 minutes introduction

12 minutes individual work

5 minutes feedback and concluding

9 Solving personal problems

⬛ On your own

When dealing with personal problems, you could get upset and then it is easy to get stuck. Use the following guidelines to help you solve a problem. Take it step by step and write your ideas in the spaces below.

Example of a problem: Imagine that your best friend seems to have lost interest in your friendship, and spends more time with someone else. You miss your friend, but don't know what is going on. Or, you fear that on your way home, you may run into the class bully, who does not like you at all.

Step 1: What is bothering you right now? Describe how you feel.

```

```

Step 2: Imagine what it would be like when everything is OK. Use the box to describe what it would be like.

```

```

Step 3: Give yourself 3 minutes to think of everything you can do to make things better. List some actions. What can you do? Can you talk to someone? Can someone assist you or simply be with you? Who should know about this?

```

```

Step 4: You are now prepared for action. What are you going to do? Remember, there could be more than one solution.

```

```

Guidelines: Activity Sheet 10

Recovering from emotional setbacks

Learning points

Asking for help is an important aspect of being a resilient learner. If you are too shy or too proud to ask for help, you slow down your own progress. This does not imply a lack of effort on your side. Taking full responsibility for your life takes effort, but also requires the wisdom to know that we are here to make a difference to other people's lives while allowing them to make a difference to ours.

Comments

1 Discuss the steps one by one, expanding on each.
2 At the end, ask the children to share their insights.

Tip

Have a tactful discussion about events that can happen to people that could be devastating and harmful, and how help from others is needed. There are stories about people who survived horrible circumstances because there was someone there to help. Afterwards, even strong survivors need to work through the emotional aspects of trauma in order to heal completely and live normal lives.

Timing

5 minutes introduction

10 minutes general discussion, going through the steps

10 minutes sharing of stories and their learning points

5 minutes concluding

10 Recovering from emotional setbacks

👥 Large group discussion

Resilient people know when to ask for help and they find out to whom they could go. When something happens to you that makes you really sad, angry or upset, it may help to talk to a person that you can trust. Once you have talked to this person, you can keep on working through difficulties on your own as well. The following steps may help you recover from difficulties.

1 Admit to yourself that you have a problem, and think of people that you trust and that you feel comfortable to talk to.

2 Talk to a person who will understand and explain what happened and how you felt. Don't try and tell everything at once. Use a few talks to work through the experience bit by bit.

3 If you feel guilty, angry and cheated, admit that to yourself. Allow yourself to really feel the emotions – if you deny the emotions, they won't go away. They simply stay there, until they have a chance to surface again. Cry, shout into a pillow, beat your fists into a pillow or take a walk, and let go of the feelings.

4 Give up feeling like a loser. Bad things that happen to you do not make you bad. Remind yourself of your good points.

5 Forgive the person or persons who made you suffer.

6 Learn useful lessons from the experience. Think what you will do differently in future.

7 Find a short answer that you will use when people ask you about this difficulty.

8 Move on with your life, and use the wisdom you have gained from working through this problem.

Adapted from Al Siebert (1996)

11 Action plan

👥👥👥 Small group activity

Do what you can, with what you have, where you are.

Theodore Roosevelt

As a small group, complete the following and add to the list as a group effort.

Problem	What to do?	Who could help? (Add telephone number where applicable)
There is a fire.		
A person gets hurt.		
Someone follows you in a building or in the street.		
A stranger offers you a lift.		
There is a car accident.		

11 *Action plan* (continued)

There is a serious accident with people who are badly hurt.		
You get lost.		
You lose your money.		
You have a serious personal problem.		
A friend has problems at home.		
You have to work on an important group project.		

11 *Action plan* (continued)

Someone in your group does not pull their weight.		
You have to make an important decision.		
You are the target of a bully. The person is older and stronger than you are.		
Your best friend is the target of a bully.		
You are a witness when a group of bullies attack a young child in your school.		

Conflict

Finding win-win solutions

Outline

Outcomes

On completion of this unit, children should have a better understanding of their upsetting emotions and notice how their emotions make them behave. To be able to handle their emotions better, children should be able to:

- describe in their own words what the word 'conflict' means.

- notice when conflict can happen.

- prevent conflict if it is possible.

- understand that each person deals with conflict in their own way.

- use different communication skills to handle conflict.

- follow certain steps when they are in conflict.

- know different ways of dealing with difficult situations.

- handle the situation when they lose in conflict.

- understand why it is important to forgive and move on.

We have an action-oriented thinking style that favours recognition, discrimination, certainty and permanence. That is the basis of the excellent technical progress that man has made (at different times in different places).

It is not difficult to imagine that a certain thinking style can be very effective for certain purposes and useless for other purposes. It may be worse than useless: it may be dangerous.

Edward De Bono (1985)

Overview

Conflict: an advanced application

In his book *The Magic of Conflict*, Thomas Crum (1987) says that 'Conflict just is.' It is a natural everyday occurrence. But, conflict has an emotional impact on most people and that is what makes it difficult to handle. Therefore the focus in this unit is to address the emotional aspects of conflict more specifically.

Conflict management from this perspective is an advanced application of many other communication and problem-solving skills. This unit therefore integrates personality styles with the skills of listening, feedback and problem solving and the emotional awareness of conflict styles, preferences and the power of forgiveness. It would be unrealistic to expect children to fully understand and apply these skills and the aim is rather to create the awareness of the skills. This is also the opportunity to set future development goals for further improvement and refinement.

Emotional needs of the age group

Based on the emotional development of learners at this age, this unit offers the opportunity to explore the role of emotions in your dealings with people.

As this age group seems to focus on 'rules' in games, the structured thinking and ground rules address this sensitivity and the unit aims to clarify the application and necessity of rules in interaction with others. The principle of democracy is applied in conflict management through the creation of equal opportunities (for example, ground rules, the art of listening, giving respectful feedback, no interrupting, looking for mutually acceptable solutions, keeping to the structure of the process and joint planning).

Conflict can spark creativity

A good team is a balanced team, that is, balanced in the sense that different members offer different viewpoints and inputs.

Once Alfred Sloan, head of General Motors, was in a board meeting, about to make an important decision. He said: 'I take it that everybody is in agreement with the decision.' And everyone nodded their heads in assent. Sloan looked around and said: 'Then I suggest we postpone the decision. Until we have some disagreement we don't understand the problem'.

Cooper and Sawaf (1998)

There is also the viewpoint that when people start to think in exactly the same way, they revert to group thinking – an approach that limits creative outcomes, initiative, leadership and innovation.

A business school in Johannesburg (South Africa) once had a huge poster on a billboard with the inscription 'If everybody thinks alike, nobody is thinking.'

Conflict management takes time

Traditionally, we took time to manage differences that caused conflict. The relationship between differences and conflict is still important and one that we will explore. However, in today's hyper-speed world pro-active strategies are now required. Waiting for a conflict to develop is, as Grandpa used to say, like locking the barn door after the cow was stolen. While conflict can be productive, it is costly and time consuming.

Geri E.H. McArdle (1995)

Cooper and Sawaf (1998) highlight the positive and constructive potential of conflict: constructive discontent, that is, being unsatisfied to the point of doing something about it. Constructive discontent is a prerequisite for growth, transformation and renewal. However, our focus on conflict often reduces the process to a struggle in proving something or somebody right or wrong. As Thomas Crum puts it in his book *The Magic of Conflict* (1998):

> In the midst of the most splendid opportunity for growing and learning that we call conflict, we spend our time grumbling, complaining, and justifying.

And

> We beat ourselves up so mercilessly in contests we have created out of our imagined need to be right, when what we really need is to take ourselves more lightly, which will enable us to move more easily to an appropriate resolution of the conflict.

Conflict styles

The following table is based on the work of Geri E.H. McArdle (1995) and IBM (1994) in which the application of different conflict management styles are explained.

Responses to conflict situations

Avoidance

When people cannot face a situation effectively or do not have the skills to resolve the conflict situation successfully, they avoid facing the issue by ignoring or denying the conflict.

Delay

Delay or diffusion strategies are aimed at underplaying or cooling off the situation, at least for the time being, to keep the issues so vague or unclear that attempts at confrontation are unlikely.

Confrontation

Confrontation involves facing conflicting issues or persons. Confrontation can be subdivided into force and negotiation strategies.

Style	Suitable situations…	Not suitable when…
Avoiding	Confronting the issue could damage your relationship and overshadow the advantages of the resolution.	You need to address the issue and bring it into the open.
Accommodating	You value the goodwill or friendship of the other person more than the facts of the issue.	You need to make inputs and to commit yourself to an issue.
Forcing	When you have limited time or when the parties involved do not favour the option.	You realize that the results of forcing will have more impact than the benefits of getting an agreement.
Compromising	Your goals are incompatible with those of the other party. When you do not find common ground.	When each of you have to give up something, both parties may feel unsatisfied, and this could impact on your self-esteem.
Collaborating	When it is important to preserve or regain good relationships. When dealing with difficult feelings or when different viewpoints are needed to find the best solution.	When you do not have the time to go about the negotiations tactfully.

- Force includes the use of physical violence (such as, slapping the other person), bribery (that is, money, favours or gifts) and deprivation (that is, withholding information, support, resources).
- Negotiation, unlike force, offers possibilities for both sides to win. The goal of negotiation is to find a workable compromise. Negotiation as a conflict resolution alternative seems to generate the most satisfying solutions.

The usual negotiating methods in the West are compromise and consensus. Compromise suggests that both sides give up something in order to gain something. Consensus means staying with that part of the proposal on which everyone has agreed – the lowest common denominator. An approach that involves making a map of the conflict terrain and then using lateral thinking to generate alternative solutions is a better way to resolve conflicts.

Edward de Bono (1985)

Structure the thinking process

It is easy to fall into the trap of pointing fingers at others, finding excuses and avoiding blame. Although it is important to analyse the problem in order to learn from the situation, it is equally important to think creatively and come up with a solution.

Step one: face the problem

1 What is wrong? What is the problem?
2 Why do we have this problem?
3 How does this problem limit us?
4 How have we failed?
5 Who is responsible?

Step two: find a solution

1 What do we want? (What is our desired outcome?)
2 What can we do to get it?
3 What have we learnt from having this situation?
4 What do we need to do next to change the situation in a positive way?
5 How will you know that you've solved this?

Forgiveness

Although conflict can make you feel uncomfortable, stressed and even exhausted at times, you sometimes need conflict to initiate growth and development. Looking back on your life, you will find examples of times when others complicated things for you, leaving you the choice to stay where you were, grumbling and blaming, or to move on – most of the time to something better.

Even when you are not so fortunate to benefit from the change, forgiveness takes the weight off your shoulders. There is tremendous power in forgiveness. On the other hand, it is equally important to have true regret and apologize when you are in the wrong. Brandon Bays, Shakti Gawain, Claude Steiner and others have written about the negative effects of regret, resentment and anger on health and relationships, as opposed to the healing powers of forgiveness. It opens up new avenues and is a crucial step towards personal growth and happiness. As US poet Walt Whitman questions:

Have you learned lessons only of those who admired you, and were tender with you, and stood aside for you? Have you not learned great lessons from those who brace themselves against you, and dispute the passage with you?

(Quoted in Cooper and Sawaf, 1998)

Guidelines
and
Activity Sheets

Guidelines: Activity Sheet 1

What is conflict?

Learning points

This activity is an attempt to address a spectrum of conflict issues like terminology, situations, actions (including body language), emotions, etc. that signifies conflict for children.

Comments

1 Start with a short role play that serves as an ice-breaker, followed by small group discussions.
2 Small group discussions result in a listing of words on the activity sheet. These can be written on the board as a summary during the general discussion.

Tip

You may find it helpful to play background music of drums or a heavy rhythm and deep sounds to convey the concept.

Timing

2 minutes role play

3 minutes small group discussions

5 minutes summarizing

2 minutes discussion about what causes fights

1 minute discussion of 'How does conflict make you feel?'

1 *What is conflict?*

👥 Small group discussion

Conflict happens when people or groups have different opinions, ideas or interests.

1 Without saying anything, each person in the group takes a turn to mime a situation in which someone is having a fight, argument or disagreement.

2 As a group, find ten words that mean 'conflict' to you.

👥 Large group discussion

1 What causes fights at home or in school?

2 How does conflict make you feel?

It's not so difficult to understand why different countries make war against each other, when we look at the huge fights in families over putting down the toilet seat.

Adapted from Thomas Crum (1987)

Guidelines: Activity Sheet 2

Conflict choices

Learning points

We have choices in terms of how we handle conflict and, depending on our own choices, or the choices others make, relationships are strengthened or damaged.

Comments

1 Ask the children to study the diagram on Activity Sheet 2 and, in a short discussion with learning partners, talk about what they observe and interpret.
2 Feedback is given to the larger group.

Tip

Put the diagram on a slide or poster for streamlining discussions.

Timing

1 minute introduction

1 minute discussion

2–3 minutes feedback to larger group with sharing of personal observations or experiences, guided by the teacher – allow extra time if children come up with relevant information or discussion points

1 minute concluding

2 Conflict choices

👥 Share in pairs   👥👥 Large group discussion

With a learning partner, discuss the meaning of the diagram above and be prepared to give feedback to the larger group.

Guidelines: Activity Sheet 3

Stages of conflict

Learning points

Conflict management should ideally include pro-active strategies to prevent the occurrence of conflict. However, if conflict does occur, it should be handled as effectively as possible. In the case of open conflict, the aim should be to minimize damage and costs.

Interpersonal conflicts can be handled more successfully if the parties involved notice 'early warning signs' such as body language and voice tone. These signs are helpful in determining the appropriate approach during conversations in stressful conflict situations.

Comments

1 Encourage small group discussions of the theory with feedback to the larger group.
2 Ask the children to identify conflict situations in the news, newspapers or books. Conflict could also be linked to history, language (in literature for instance) or other subjects dealing with conflict or elements of conflict and negotiations around issues.
3 Ask children to consider the question 'How do I handle conflict?' This part of the activity helps to sensitize learners to the rest of the skills addressed in the unit.
4 Large group discussion about how individuals react during conflict.

Timing

1 minute introduction to the theory

2 minutes sharing in groups

2 minutes large group discussion

1 minute introduction and explanation of the diagram

1 minute self-reflection on conflict style

3 minutes general discussion – allow extra time for spontaneous contributions or if valuable insights emerge during the discussions

3 Stages of conflict

👥👤 Theory

Expecting conflict

When there are changes in the way we do things, or when we have different ideas of how something should be done, we may expect somebody to stand up and complain or even insist that things should be done in a different way. This could happen for instance when school rules change, new subjects are introduced or school hours are adjusted.

Discussing matters

When people are aware of the tension between them, they may make jokes about the issue and pretend that it is not serious. This is often the first sign that something more serious could happen and arguments may develop.

Open conflict

This is when people are so upset that they argue with each other, and even say hurtful things to each other or about each other. During open conflict, each person may strive to win at the cost of the other person.

👤 On your own

How do I handle conflict?

Which style do you use most often? What feels like 'you'?

Collaborating	Accommodating	Avoiding	Compromising	Forcing
Finding a solution that suits both parties even if it takes time.	Giving up your ideas to please the other person.	Pretending the conflict does not exist.	Everybody gives something up to reach an agreement.	Wants to win at all costs and is competitive.

Inspired by *Working Smarter: The Learner Within* (IBM, 1994)

Guidelines: Activity Sheet 4

How people handle conflict

Learning points

People can have different approaches to conflict based on personality types, upbringing, nature of the conflict, etc.

Comments

1 Refer to the different approaches to conflict. Ask for personal interpretation or opinions about the different conflict styles.
2 Lead a general discussion on how appropriate each style is, depending on the situation and relationship with the other party. For example, sensitive personal issues could benefit from delay while crucial issues need to be addressed irrespective of how difficult or uncomfortable it makes the opposing parties feel.
3 Point out the importance of tact and good discretion in choosing the right time, place and approach when addressing the issue.
4 Explain the potential harm that aggression can do to relationships and teamwork, and how long it takes to heal relationships and regain trust.

Timing

1 minute introduction

4 minutes general discussion with the teacher guiding the discussion by working through the activity sheet with the children

4 *How people handle conflict*

👥 Theory

Avoid   **Delay**   **Confront**

Read the explanations below of the different ways people deal with conflict. Then draw a picture to illustrate each one in the boxes on the right.

Avoid

They pretend that there is no conflict and they do not talk about it or do anything about it.

Delay

They want to deal with the conflict, but not now, so they put it off until later. They simply postpone the conflict and even wish it would go away in the meantime.

Confront

They deal directly with the conflict and try to solve the problem. But some people will try to win at all costs, while others will talk about the differences in order to find a solution that will keep the friendship going.

👥 Small group discussion

1 What do you do when there is conflict in your house or between you and a friend?
2 What do you notice about your friend's reactions?
3 What happens in your family when there is conflict?

Guidelines: Activity Sheet 5

Taking personal conflict step by step

Learning points

Children can learn to solve their own problems by calmly and systematically working through the different steps on Activity Sheet 5. It teaches them to think for themselves and arrive at solutions with which they feel comfortable.

Comments

1 Introduce the topic by asking the children to think of a very important decision they have to make, or something that is bothering them at the moment, or a while ago.
2 Each child then sits alone with enough private space and works through the problem. This could also be done at home.
3 The only sharing in the group is about the usefulness of the approach, and whether they have learnt something or gained insight during the activity.

Timing

1 minute introduction and explanation that the activity equals 'alone time'

4–7 minutes individual work, depending on work pace of children

3 minutes discussion of the value of structured thinking, and the control it gives you over your life and situations – allow extra time if a lively discussion warrants it

5 *Taking personal conflict step by step*

👤 On your own

When we have personal problems, it is easy to get stuck. One way of dealing with a difficult decision is to take it step by step. Write your ideas in the spaces below.

STEP 1: What is bothering you right now?

```
```

STEP 2: Imagine what it would be like when everything is perfect. Describe what it would be like.

```
```

STEP 3: How can you change your situation – in other words, what can you do to solve the problem? Give yourself a few minutes to think of everything you can do to make things better. List your ideas in the box below.

```
```

STEP 4: You are now ready for action. Write down the first action you are going to take to solve the problem and achieve your goal.

```
```

Guidelines: Activity Sheet 6

Count to ten

Learning points

Impulse control is an important emotional tool for ensuring that responses are useful, productive and true to ourselves. It relates to a sense of timing, delay of gratification, and self-management and self-mastery. Eventually it also contributes to positive self-esteem.

Comments

1. Use Activity Sheet 6 as a guide, and have a short general discussion on the topic.
2. Ask the children to think about times when they felt like biting their tongue, regretted losing their temper, did something without thinking, or acted in frustration.

Timing

1 minute introduction

3 minutes teacher slowly reading through the reflection, giving children time to reflect/think – children do not respond verbally

1 minute short summary by teacher and asking children to think of a situation during which this approach would have been a better solution.

6 Count to ten

When we have strong emotions, we forget to think!

> Anyone can become angry – that is easy. But to be angry with the right person, to the right degree, at the right time, for the right purpose, and in the right way – this is not easy.
>
> *Aristotle*

👤 Reflection

Think of a time, when you were very angry, and you did something that did not feel like the real you.

- What happened?

- What did you do?

- Why did you feel like that?

- If you had the opportunity to be in that same situation again, what would you do differently?

Notice that you have just spent some moments thinking things over before you have answered the last question in your own mind/silently. So next time you are upset, do the following:

1 Wait – count to ten

2 Breathe

3 Calm down

4 Think

5 Speak and act!

Test your response by asking yourself: 'If I say what I feel right now, will I be breaking or will I be building relationships and my self-esteem?' Sometimes it is better not to say anything at all, and walk away until you have calmed down and thought about the situation. Then go back with a response that you feel comfortable with and will be fair towards the other person.

Talk tactfully

Learning points

This activity is an application of feedback skills and the use of WIN-messages. The principle is that the talker owns the message. It is not blaming, attacking or complaining, but rather a description of the talker's experience of the event.

Comments

1 The children work in pairs and formulate answers.
2 They give feedback to the larger group.

Tip

Children are still in the process of developing emotional skills, and may find this activity difficult. It may be useful to begin with several general examples. Be sensitive not to refer to 'wrong' or 'right' answers, but instead assist in refining skills. This is not an easy skill to master.

Timing

Depending on the size of the group, it may take up to a minute per participating pair.

7 Talk tactfully

👥 Share in pairs

Work in pairs and for each of the examples below, write one of your own. Be prepared to read your examples to the larger group and take care not to use examples that may hurt or embarrass others.

1 Show that you understand the other person's feelings. You might not agree, but when you understand and accept the other person, you make it easier for the other person to relax and talk.

Example:
'I can understand that you are upset. If I were in your position, I might feel the same.'

2 Accept it when the other person does not feel comfortable to talk about the problem. Later on, the person might feel like sharing information.

Example:
'I understand that some things are private. You do not need to discuss that now.'

3 Use 'I' messages. Describe actions, feelings and effects, not the person.

Example:
'When you did not return my call, I thought that you were angry at me.'
Not:
'You never phone back.'

Guidelines: Activity Sheet 8

Listen to understand

Learning points

To listen to the extent that you really understand how the other person feels. To check for understanding by repeating what you think the person has said. (Paraphrasing – putting it in your own words.)

Comments

1 Hand out newspaper clippings about conflict-related situations and encourage the children to read through them.
2 The children may read through more than one, and decide for themselves which articles they want to use as inspiration for the role play or whether they want to use their own examples.
3 The children relate their interpretation of a conflict situation during the role play.
4 The children decide who starts, but each child gets an opportunity to be talker, listener and observer.
5 Indicate when the role playing starts and stops, and inform groups that they will have 2 minutes per round of role playing and 2 minutes of sharing experiences.
6 After about 2 minutes of role playing, instruct the groups to stop and share their experiences as either a listener, an observer or a talker and what was difficult about the role.
7 Ask the children to switch roles, and again give them 2 minutes for role play and 2 minutes for feedback.
8 At the end of the activity, one child should be invited to give feedback to the larger group on the experiences of the group as a whole.
9 At the end, de-role the children.
10 List learning points on the board for all to see.

Tip

This is not easy, so do not expect perfection. It is fine if this is an area for further development.

Timing

5 minutes for organizing groups and distributing clippings

1–2 minutes silent reading for the storyteller

2 minutes role playing × 3

2 minutes feedback time × 3

5 minutes feedback to the larger group

1 minute summarizing

8 Listen to understand

👥👥👥 Listening and feedback

Storyteller	Active Listener	Observer
Use a newspaper article that really interests you, or that you find very disturbing. Tell the others what you think about it.	Listen to the storyteller and find out as much as possible about the person's feelings. Try understanding the person's feelings.	Carefully notice what the listener does. Use the table below to judge the listener's skills. Explain to the listener how you have rated him/her, using the table below.

Rating: Needs work (1)   Good (2)   Excellent (3)

Rate your partner as a listener, using the questionnaire below. Be prepared to give feedback to your learning partner once you have completed the role play.

1 Made sure that he/she understood what the other person had said by repeating the storyteller's story in his/her own words.	☐
2 Named the storyteller's feelings.	☐
3 Did not agree or disagree.	☐
4 Did not give advice.	☐
5 Talked back in a way that was easy to understand.	☐
6 Did not interrupt.	☐
7 Asked good questions.	☐
8 Said 'hmmm' or 'uh-uh' to make the other person feel more comfortable.	☐
9 Looked the person in the eye.	☐
10 Nodded head.	☐
11 Leaned forward.	☐
12 Did not wave hands or keep them too still.	☐
13 Turned body towards the speaker.	☐

Repeat the exercise three times so that everyone has the opportunity to practise being the Storyteller, the Listener and the Observer.

👥👥👥👥 Comments

Discuss what you have learnt in the larger group.

Guidelines: Activity Sheet 9

More ideas

Learning points

Confronting is not the only way to respond to conflict, and it may be wise to use different tactics. Apologizing takes courage and is an important social skill. Highly resilient individuals can admit mistakes because they have a strong self-esteem.

Comments

Short general discussion. Using examples of people who publicly apologized may be a good way to introduce the subject. Ask the children how they feel about public apologies.

Tip

Important: when apologizing, it is important to show true regret as well as improved behaviour afterwards.

Timing

1 minute introduction of the topic

5 minutes general discussion about the importance of apologizing and sharing opinions about different situations where apologies are appropriate

2 minutes summarizing learning points

1 minute conclusion

9 *More ideas*

👥 Theory

If a team of soldiers charge towards a closed door with a battering ram, and someone opens the door at the precise moment that the soldiers reach the door, what would happen? They would fall flat on their faces!'

Pienaar and Spoelstra (1992)

Apologize

Sometimes we can avoid a fight from becoming even worse by saying: 'I am sorry.' Most people will accept it if we really are sorry.

Say goodbye

If you've tried everything to make peace, but the other person stays angry, just walk away.

Stay quiet

Sometimes it is best to keep quiet and not say anything at all.

👥 Small group discussion

Silence: absolute silence, with no response at all, could be very powerful.

Pienaar and Spoelstra (1992)

What else could you do? Write notes or make a drawing of a possible solution in the box below.

Guidelines: Activity Sheet 10

Work according to a plan

Learning points

Because we are upset when we are in conflict situations, it helps to work systematically according to a recipe.

Comments

1 Introduce the topic to pairs.
2 Pairs try the activity by themselves, and give feedback to the larger group.

Timing

10–15 minutes playing time

2 minutes de-roling and summarizing

10 *Work according to a plan*

👥 In pairs

When you have a disagreement with a friend or classmate, ask the person whether you could meet for a friendly conversation. It is possible that the other person may not want to do it, or may not be ready for such a discussion, so don't be too disappointed if your suggestion is not accepted. Don't try and force your idea on the other person. It may be a good idea to wait a little longer before you talk to the person directly. However, don't keep on postponing the discussion.

Example:
You find yourself disagreeing with your best friend in a discussion in your class. You end up biting your lip and not saying what you really think and need to talk to your friend.

Step 1:   Find a quiet place where you can talk about your differences without being interrupted

1 Say why you are meeting.

2 Say that you want to make peace.

3 Decide what the rules are. For instance:

   ● Only one person talks at a time

   ● No swearing

   ● No finger pointing

   ● No shouting

4 Say that you hope you can work things out.

Write in the box below where a good place to meet would be. Also write down the first sentence you would say when you sit down with your friend. (How would you greet your friend and what would be your first sentence to get the conversation going?)

```



```

Step 2:   Describe what the problem is and how you feel about it

1 Each person tells his or her side of the story while the other person listens.

2 Repeat what you think the other person has said.

3 Remember, it is best if you:

   ● talk only about what really happened.

10 *Work according to a plan* (continued)

- avoid name-calling.

- use WIN messages (for example, 'When you walked away, I felt confused, because I did not understand the reason for your behaviour').

- listen to understand the other person's point of view.

- show that you are listening.

- do not interrupt even if you don't agree with everything the person says while the person is talking.

- talk only when it is your turn.

Write down how you will show that you really listen to your friend, even though you may not agree with everything he or she says?

Step 3: Decide what both of you would like to happen

1 Say what you both want.

2 Talk about what may happen if you don't make peace.

3 Remember nobody needs to be 'guilty'. We all make mistakes. Rather concentrate on how to improve.

Write down some of the things that could happen if you don't make peace.

Step 4: Come up with ideas to solve the problem

1 Make a list of all the things you can think of that will help you work together and solve the problem.

10 *Work according to a plan* (continued)

Write down your ideas for solving the problem.

Step 5:   Select a possible solution

1 Decide which plan will work best for both of you.

2 Promise each other to try and stick to your solution.

How are you going to decide which plan is the best? Describe how you will go about it. (For example, you could discuss each idea on the list before choosing one. What else can you do to choose the best solution?)

Step 6:   Decide what to do

1 Decide how you are going to make it work.

2 Write down how you can ensure that each person will keep his or her promise.

Guidelines: Activity Sheet 11

Be careful when another person gets violent

Learning points

It helps to be aware of the warning signs and have alternative ideas of how to handle the situation. It is best if you are not taken by surprise when someone gets extremely agitated.

Comments

1 Short overview and general discussion precedes the activity. Ask two or three pairs of children to mime a violent situation before the larger group. Instruct them not to make any physical contact, and to maintain complete silence. They are allowed to use body language only. De-role at the end.

2 Next, instruct the children to each express their idea of conflict in the space provided at the top of the activity sheet. Alternatively, small groups can make posters about violence. Children are free to write down words, draw symbols, make drawings, or create collages with pictures, words and their own drawings to make a representation of the concept of violence. They may use newspaper or magazine clippings supplied by the teacher. Children can also be briefed beforehand to bring their own material for classroom work.

3 Go through the theory and give the children the opportunity to add their own suggestions for dealing effectively with violence.

Tip

Quietly observe behaviour during the activity in order to identify individuals who may need professional help and need to be referred to sources of support. It is essential to be discreet and show respect for privacy and difficult emotions. Be prepared to handle emotional situations should they occur.

Timing

1 minute introduction

4 minutes role play with de-roling at the end

20 minutes illustrating the experience or concept of violence in the classroom

10 minutes discussing the artwork and complimenting children on aspects of their creations

5 minutes working through the theory on the worksheet in a large group discussion and generating more ideas for handling violent situations effectively

1 minute conclusion

11 *Be careful when another person gets violent*

♟ On your own

Illustrate your impression of violence in the box below. You may use words, colour, symbols, drawings or a collage of pictures or words.

♟♟♟♟ Theory

Watch out for signs. If it looks as if the person is going to attack you, decide where and how you could escape.

- Stay calm – breathe deeply.

- Speak calmly and hold your body still.

- Avoid touching a very angry person.

- Suggest that you move to a place with lots of space.

- Show that you are listening.

- Avoid telling the person what you think he/she is trying to do. Remember, you cannot read another person's mind.

- Sometimes it could help if you could make a joke, but be careful, it may make the person even more angry.

Guidelines: Activity Sheet 12

When it is over, it is over!

Learning points

Forgiveness is a very powerful emotional skill and is particularly relevant in mental health. Highly resilient people do not bear grudges.

Comments

A child reads the story and the lesson is shortly pointed out.

Timing

2–3 minutes for reading and discussion

12 *When it is over, it is over!*

When a fight is over, it is important to let go of all your negative emotions. If you do not forgive, you will keep on reminding the other person of things that are best left behind.

👤👤👤👤 Story

Late one afternoon, two monks were hurrying to get home before dark. On their way home, they met a beautiful young woman who had to cross the river to get to her home. The woman looked anxiously at the deep water, and exclaimed: 'How will I ever be able to cross the river? The water is so high!' The taller monk decided to help. He hoisted the woman on his back, quickly crossed the river and put her down on the other side. She thanked him, and went on her way home.

The monks continued their journey. Suddenly the shorter monk said angrily: 'You know you are not supposed to touch a woman!' He went on reprimanding his friend because it is considered improper for a monk to touch a lady.

The taller monk just listened for a while. Then he interrupted the long speech and said: 'Excuse me, my brother, I left the lady by the river hours ago. Are you still carrying her?'

👤👤👤👤 Large group discussion

Does forgiving also mean forgetting?

Guidelines: Activity Sheet 13

When you lose a fight

Learning points

Dealing with anger, frustration, humiliation and disappointment in a productive way is a form of stress prevention.

Comments

General large group discussion with tips from the group.

Timing

2 minutes

13 *When you lose a fight*

♟♟♟♟ Large group discussion

We cannot always be winners. If you lose, try the following:

1 Exercise, take a walk, cycle, etc. to relieve stress and take your mind of it.

2 Instead of being angry at yourself, learn from your mistakes. Think how you will act next time the same type of thing happens.

3 Just let go of the negative feelings and thoughts.

4 Take a walk in a beautiful park or garden.

5 Talk to a friend.

6 Share with the rest of the group your solution for dealing with uncomfortable emotions when you lose a fight.

14 *Action plan*

 On your own

I would like to...	Tick here
1 Learn to count to ten before I respond	☐
2 Think before I talk	☐
3 Really listen to understand	☐
4 Make sure of the facts	☐
5 Forgive others when they hurt me or differ from me	☐
6 Forgive myself for mistakes	☐
7 Give honest but tactful feedback	☐
8 Prepare myself to deal with conflict	☐
9 Check for understanding	☐
10 Respect others' viewpoints even if I don't agree	☐
11 Accept the situations I cannot change	☐
12 Learn not to take things personally	☐
13 Choose the right time to talk about differences	☐
14 Put myself in the other people's shoes, to understand how they feel and why they feel the way they do.	☐

Once you have marked the items in the list, be prepared to give feedback to the larger group – if you feel comfortable to do so. Notice how some people share the same challenge.

Money matters

I am taking care of my money

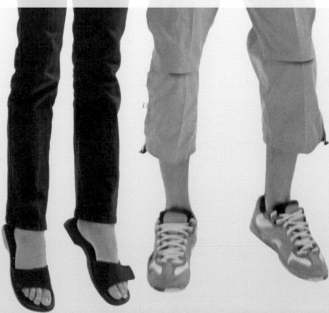

Outline

Outcomes

On completion of this unit, children should have the knowledge, skills and attitudes to:

- describe how they feel about money as a resource.

- understand how to determine their own financial worth.

- draw up a basic budget to understand what money is needed for.

- engage their family in discussions around money and its role in their lives.

- list typical household expenses in their family.

- understand how to use money as a resource.

- find ways to spend money more wisely.

- look for ways to save money.

- understand that some things are valuable to people but may not have financial worth.

- explain why it is important to save money for future needs and wants.

Ideally, children should report back on their financial progress after one or two months and share practical advice with learning partners.

Don't worry about how the future will turn out; it is out of your control. Think about what you're going to do now to get where you want to be in your future.

Bernice Cohen (1999)

Overview

Beliefs about money

A healthy attitude towards money is crucial for achieving financial freedom. Your beliefs about money determine your attitude towards money and in turn influence what you do with your money. If you believe that money is the root of all evil, you will handle it very differently from if you see it as a source of energy – a means of getting what you need and want in life.

- If you focus too much on money at the expense of relationships and health, you become the slave of money.
- If you have too little of it, you constantly worry about money, so money is all you think about!
- By being in control of your finances, you create financial freedom for yourself, and then money takes its rightful place in the totality of your life.

Hopefully we all have dreams and aspirations – many of which will cost money to realize. Having the right attitude towards money is therefore crucial in the process of self-actualization and the achievement of personal and career success.

The ideal is to have enough money and let it work for you. Although money is an important or powerful asset, it is complementary to human capital, which is priceless.

Contributing

A 10-year-old boy went into a coffee shop for an ice cream. As he sat down to order, he asked for the price of an ice cream with a topping. The waitress gave him the price. Instead of ordering, he took some coins out of his pocket and started counting. The waitress had to serve other customers as well and started to become edgy.

Looking up, the boy asked for the price of an ice cream without a topping. By now the waitress was highly irritated and grudgingly gave him the price. The boy ordered the plain ice cream. When the waitress returned with the order she brusquely placed it in front of the boy and immediately turned her attention to the other customers.

The boy finished his ice cream and left. However, when the waitress started to clear his table, she had to blink twice and swallow hard. There, placed neatly beside the plate, were a few coins – her tip!

The moral of this story is that some people are naturally more sharing and understand how to live within their means in order to make other contributions as well. This is an attitude that can be developed in children.

(Adapted from Canfield and Hansen, 2000)

Financial worth

What happens when employees have financial difficulties? How are families affected by financial issues?

People grappling with money problems experience:

- stress
- frustration
- low energy levels
- poor self-esteem
- difficulty with relationships
- family hardship.

On the other hand, financial stability could contribute towards:

- feelings of competence and achievement
- self-confidence
- personal empowerment
- peace of mind
- higher energy levels and productivity
- relaxed, quality family time
- enjoyment of life
- healthier lifestyle.

For many people, the difference between assets and belongings with pure sentimental value are not that clear. Sometimes people buy items for amusement or status while they forget that some assets or investments increase in value while other items rapidly lose their market value.

Teaching children the principles of sound financial management has long-term positive implications. While money matters affect emotional well-being, they also influence the resilience of individuals, families and communities. To be in control of your finances and provide for the unforeseen and the future is to experience true financial freedom.

Drawing up a budget

The principles of impulse control (to resist the temptation to act immediately) and delay of gratification (to wait to satisfy a want) are extremely relevant in terms of how and when you spend your money.

Children who borrow money from parents to buy things could easily land in the credit trap. The sooner they understand the principle of living within their means, the earlier they will experience financial freedom – freedom from overdrafts, credit card debt and all sorts of financial burdens that could make their lives miserable if not controlled and handled with discretion.

Providing for future needs and wants

For most young people, old age is something in the distant future. However, most old people will agree that old age catches up with you sooner than you expect. To really have a fulfilling life in old age, you need to make provision for it. Many of the things that make life more comfortable and enjoyable, such as sharing a dinner with family, cost money.

Saving as a habit

Consider how financial decisions made during a person's twenties can affect the rest of their life. Compound interest makes a staggering difference to

what they will have in the bank at the age of 50, 60 or 80. The sooner young people start thinking about money and learn to manage money properly, the sooner they can direct their actions towards self-sufficiency.

Adding value

Do you know exactly what you are worth in monetary terms? Whether you work for a large company or a small business, you need to ensure that you add value. Many companies encourage intrapreneurship (like an entrepreneur, but inside a company). This means that as an employee you take responsibility for the productivity and financial viability of a particular department, which functions as a profit centre. You actually run the department like a self-sufficient business unit.

The value you add could also be measured in terms of the quality of the relationships with team members and customers. In the long term, selling and doing business is all about good relationships and giving value for money – going the extra mile for the client, putting in extra effort to make sure the client is happy, and making sure the client is satisfied and gets a fair deal. In fact, it is when customers get more than what they bargained for that they really become loyal long-term clients. They will advertise the business by word of mouth and thereby ensure the survival of the company.

As a teacher, what are your views on the value you are adding? Are the children and parents, as customers of your school, advertising the school by word of mouth based on their satisfaction?

Being pro-active

Being financially pro-active means that you:

- have a clear future vision.
- have specific financial goals and time frames.

- work according to a budget.
- engage your family members as supporters of your financial plan.
- live within your means.
- plan how to make and spend your hard earned money.
- save money.
- have a variety of assets and investments – you do not keep all your resources in one place.
- ensure that you also enjoy your money responsibly.
- celebrate financial successes when you reach a target!

Good luck with your efforts!

Guidelines
and
Activity Sheets

Guidelines: Activity Sheet 1

My beliefs about money

Learning points

Money is an emotional issue – just think what happens when something impacts on your finances! Finances affect various other areas of your life negatively or positively, depending on your attitude towards money and the skills you apply when dealing with financial resources. What you believe about money will determine how you will go about your handling of money.

Comments

1 As an ice-breaker, use some newspaper clippings to start a conversation in the large group. Ask for opinions and allow the sharing of personal experience.
2 Instruct the children to sit in groups of four or five to work through the activity sheet. Each child makes short notes on the activity sheet while addressing questions.
3 At the end of the small group discussion, feedback is given to the larger group. Each question should be handled individually, with feedback from all the groups, before moving on to the next question.
4 Close the discussion with a summary of the group's discussions and learning points.

Tip

Use newspaper clippings on personal finance relating to:

- family fights over money.
- inheritance of property and how people handle the issues.
- articles describing emotional turmoil in families over inheritance of property or other issues related to money. In extreme cases even suicide related to financial problems.
- lottery winners.
- financial mismanagement.
- financial successes.

Timing

10 minutes ice-breaker

20 minutes discussion time

10 minutes feedback and concluding

1 *My beliefs about money*

👥 Small group discussion

Discuss the following questions within a small group. Be prepared to give feedback to the larger group.

1 When do you consider a person to be rich?

2 How much money is 'enough' for a person of your age? Give the reasons for your answer.

3 Do you personally know a person whom you admire as a very good business person? What makes you think that the person is a good business person?

4 Do you know a person who really handles money well? Explain to the group why you think the person knows how to work with money. What can you learn from this person?

5 When is a job a 'good job'? Discuss your viewpoints within your small group.

6 What kind of job would you like to do when you leave school? Why?

Guidelines: Activity Sheet 2

My own financial worth

Learning points

The aim of this activity is to help children understand the difference between assets with financial or monetary worth and belongings with sentimental value. This knowledge will encourage children to carefully consider options before they make purchases. It is said that people with credit cards are inclined to spend up to 30 per cent more compared to what they spend when they use cash only. Using credit or borrowing money can therefore give you a false sense of security and entice you into overspending.

Comments

1 The children complete the activity sheet on their own, and report back to the larger group.
2 Conclude the discussion with a few general comments or a summary of the individual responses.

Timing

3 minutes briefing

10 minutes working individually

5 minutes discussion time and concluding

2 *My own financial worth*

🯄 On your own

You are very valuable as a person. It is important that you always remind yourself that you have lots of potential and that you are special and unique. There is nobody else in the world exactly like you and therefore your needs will be different from everybody else's. In the world of work and finances though, we are measured by what we have – our assets. Assets are things that can be measured in terms of money. Read the list below and fill in what you think is the correct value in money.

What am I worth, money wise?

My possessions/What I own	Value in money
How much money do you have with you right now?	
If you have a bank account, how much money is in your account?	
In the space below write a list of your belongs, such as a bicycle, sports equipment, toys, games, etc., then in the column on the right fill in what they are worth (at what price would someone be willing to buy them).	
Are you willing to sell some of your belongings? Yes/No	
Do you think you will find a buyer for the things you are willing to sell? Yes/No	
How much money will a person be willing to pay for the things you want to sell? Write you answer in the column on the right.	

What I owe	Value in money
Have you borrowed money from your parents or somebody else? If so, how much?	
Have you promised someone else something that you still need to deliver? If so, how much is it going to cost you?	

If you owe more than what you have or possess, you could benefit from a personal budget and a personal financial plan. You will find the information in the next few activity sheets particularly useful to you.

Guidelines: Activity Sheet 3

Take stock

Learning points

When you respect and appreciate your belongings, you are more inclined to keep them in order and under your control. By keeping only what you need, you can give to others while being thankful for what you have. Some people find it difficult to get rid of things and live in clutter – surrounded by items they no longer use. Sometimes useful objects like household gadgets lie around unutilized, which is a waste of resources. Although monetary worth is important, it is necessary to live a balanced life and develop different aspects of your life while you enjoy what you have.

Comments

1 Ask the children what their favourite things are, with each child having the opportunity to share this information with the larger group. Point out the difference between monetary value and sentimental value.
2 This activity could be completed at home and reported back to the group, with emphasis on the personal experience of the child.

Timing

15 minutes discussion after home play

3 *Take stock*

👤 Home play

By tidying your room properly, you could feel more in control of your belongings and you could look properly after the things you really care about. Follow the steps and see what a difference it makes to your life.

Step one

Carefully look through your belongings. Collect everything you know you should get rid of. This includes useless items that are simply gathering dust. Put these items in one place until you have finished your room. Now throw them away!

Step two

Carefully check your room and storage space again. This time collect every bit of money you can find and put it in a jar. Put a list of the things you really want on the jar. This is to remind you that saving money will get you there!

Step three

When you go through your room this time, collect everything that is still usable, but not of value to you anymore. Put it in a neat bag and give it to somebody who can make good use of it.

Step four

Go through your room a final time. Take note of the things you care about and that you feel are valuable to you. They may not be valuable to anybody else. Sit down for a few minutes and feel thankful for what you have.

Make a drawing of something you value in the space at the bottom of the page. Share with the group why this object is special to you.

Guidelines: Activity Sheet 4

Drawing up a budget

Learning points

Many children do not understand how complex or extensive the needs of a household can be. By working out a budget for a school event, they learn about hidden costs and the discipline needed to reach a target. The expectation should not be to have a perfect budget first time, but rather that the children learn from each other, ask questions about others' ideas and present their ideas to a group. This activity could lead to a discussion of the principle of budgeting at home and could potentially facilitate family conversations.

The activity stimulates:

- an understanding how each project has financial implications, similar to running a household.
- an appreciation of parent's efforts and possible sacrifices for the benefit of their children.
- an awareness of personal future needs.

Comments

1 Discuss the meaning of the word budget. (A simple explanation could be that a budget is a plan according to which you make, use and save money.)
2 Why have a budget? (To take control of your money and to know where it goes. Without a budget you might spend money unwisely, which could lead to financial troubles.)
3 Discuss in the large group the advantages and disadvantages of using different strategies for handling money.
4 Instruct the large group to divide into small groups and work out a budget, with a scribe making notes on a sheet of paper or flipchart.
5 Each small group presents to the larger group, explaining their reasoning.

Timing

5 minutes briefing

10 minutes role play

10 minutes drawing up a budget

10 minutes small groups presenting to the larger group

5 minutes concluding

4 *Drawing up a budget*

♟♟♟ Small and large group

Discuss the following questions in your small group and prepare to give feedback to the larger group.

I   What is a budget? Write your group's definition of a budget in the box below.

```



```

2   Why is it important to have a budget? Share your opinion with the large group.

♟♟♟ Role play: draw up a school project budget

As a group of friends, you have all decided that you want to go on a school trip as it will be your last opportunity to be together during a fun school event before going to different secondary schools.

- You know about the trip a year (12 months) beforehand.

- The total cost is £600.

- Your parents will contribute £450.

- You have to find a way to raise the remainder – £150.

- What is the best way of handling a budget for a school trip?

Debate the following options within your group, choose one option, and use it for a role play.

- Let the most responsible person in the group handle the budget on behalf of the group.

- In the beginning of the project, decide how you are going to save or make money and, as you progress, put the money in different envelopes, each with the amount and purpose written on it, and keep it somewhere safe until it is needed.

- Sit together as a group/team and decide how you are going to save and manage your money, drawing up a budget beforehand.

The challenge is to plan in advance, and ensure that you have enough money for the tour. Each member has to take part in the discussion. Once you have decided how you are going to raise the money and manage the combined budget, you have to write down your scheme on a sheet of flipchart paper and present it to the larger group. Be prepared to answer questions about your budget. Feel free to ask questions of other groups about their budgets, once each group has had the opportunity to present their budgets to the larger group.

Guidelines: Activity Sheet 5

Spending habits

Learning points

You can easily form habits of spending money without seriously considering the necessity of things. Group or peer pressure often leads children to try to keep up with a current fashionable image. Eventually you have to decide what is really important to you. How often have you succumbed to the urge to buy something only to find that it did not 'live up' to expectations?

Comments

1 Introduce the topic by asking the children what is 'in' and what is a must to be fashionable.
2 Ask them about useless items gathering dust that were once considered necessities.
3 Each child completes the self-assessment on Activity Sheet 5 and feedbacks to the larger group.
4 Conclude with the question: 'What have you learnt from doing this activity?

Timing

5–10 minutes for introduction

10 minutes self-assessment

5 minutes feedback

5 Spending habits

👥 Share in pairs

On your own, read through the following list and then tick items that are true for your household. Then discuss the list with a learning partner. At the end of the activity, you may decide to share the results with the large group and your family at home.

Do you:

1 Have a cellular phone? Do you know how much it costs per year? ☐

2 Buy fancy ice cream, cookies and sweets instead of ordinary ones? ☐

3 Own appliances that you seldom use? (bread-maker, popcorn popper, etc.) ☐

4 Own expensive equipment like cameras, TVs, VCRs, etc.? ☐

5 Often buy CDs? ☐

6 Go on expensive holidays? ☐

7 Take clothes to the dry cleaner that you could clean yourself? ☐

8 Buy sliced bread, instead of basic brown bread? ☐

9 Buy convenience foods and take-aways? ☐

10 Drink expensive bottled water and juices? ☐

11 Buy expensive fashionable shoes? ☐

12 Buy high fashion items early in the season? ☐

13 Often pay late charges on videos and library books? ☐

14 Buy bargains even when you do not necessarily need the item immediately? ☐

15 Own expensive gadgets or items to impress friends or peers? ☐

16 Fail to look after your belongings properly? ☐

17 Discard clothes simply because you like the newer items more? ☐

👥👥 Large group discussion

What else can you add to the list above? Write your suggestion(s) in the box below.

[ ]

Guidelines: Activity Sheet 6

Cut down unnecessary expenses

Learning points

By consciously thinking about what you have and why you have it, you could work out how you spend money on unnecessary items.

Comments

1 Instruct the children to do this activity at home.
2 During the next session they share the outcomes in pairs.
3 Individuals give feedback to the group. Acknowledge those who have done the work at home and the contribution of ideas and tips.
4 Lead a general discussion and list learning points on the board.

Tip

You could list unnecessary items on a separate sheet of paper or flipchart (or in a separate column on the board), and tear up the paper and discard it. (You could wipe clean the list of unnecessary items for the same reason.) This will demonstrate how wasteful unnecessary items are.

Timing

5 minutes short introductory explanation and orientation

15 minutes discussion and highlighting learning points

6 Cut down unnecessary expenses

👤 Home play with feedback to the larger group

Use the table to write down some of the items you regularly buy in your household. Decide whether the items are really needed, whether you could buy less, or whether you could even skip some items!

Expense item	Needed	Buy less	Skip

Keep on looking for ways to save money!

Guidelines: Activity Sheet 7

My personal needs, wants and values

Learning points

This activity encourages self-reflection and the development of a sound personal value system. Although children in this age group still have to follow rules and their parents' instructions and guidelines, they are starting to separate their identities from those of their parents, and therefore need to form personal values.

Comments

1 Clarify the terminology: needs (things you cannot do without); wants (things that are nice to have, but not necessities); values (things that are important to you and that you would not easily give up; values help you to decide how right your decisions and actions are).
2 The children complete the self-assessment on Activity Sheet 7 on their own.
3 Each child has the opportunity to share the outcomes of the activity with the group.
4 Point out that values are personal, but the needs of others are also important.

Tip

Although all of us have value systems, not all value systems support the common good. Eventually everything you do, even using money, reflects a value system.

Timing

5 minutes introduction

5 minutes discussing terminology

5 minutes self-assessment

15 minutes individual feedback and open discussion

7 My personal needs, wants and values

👥 Large group discussion

1. When is something a 'need', and when is it a 'want'?
2. What is a 'value'?

👤 On your own

Read through the following list and tick the items that are important to you. You may even add to the list.

My needs, wants and values	Tick
1 Spending time with family	☐
2 Spending time with friends just chatting	☐
3 Doing interesting or exciting things	☐
4 Enjoying nature	☐
5 Buying nice clothes	☐
6 Going out with friends	☐
7 Saving money in the bank	☐
8 Making money by making and selling things	☐
9 Visiting interesting places	☐
10 Doing well at school	☐
11 Taking part in sports	☐
12 Helping at home	☐
13 Caring for others	☐
14 Playing with a pet	☐
15	
16	
17	
18	
19	
20	

Ask yourself: How many of the items in your list cost money?

Guidelines: Activity Sheet 8

Eight steps to drawing up a personal budget

Learning points

Drawing up a first budget may be a daunting task. The guidelines may help you to go about it, but expect to improvise later on.

Comments

Use Activity Sheet 8 to guide a general group discussion.

Tip

This activity sheet offers the guidelines for using Activity Sheet 9, and serves to clarify terminology and concepts. While Activity Sheet 8 offers the theoretical background, Activity Sheet 9 facilitates the practical application of the theory.

Timing

10 minutes discussion

8 Eight steps to drawing up a personal budget

👤 Individual activity for group session of home play

1 Use the table on Activity Sheet 9 to work out your personal budget. Write the date at the top of the table.

2 First calculate your total income (pocket money and money you earn elsewhere).

3 Write down the amount of money you put aside as savings. This you do not use at all.

4 List everything you buy and write down what it costs under 'Amount.'

5 Indicate whether the item is a need or a want. N = Need. W = Want.

6 Add up all your expenses. This is the Total Expenditure

7 Add together your figures for Total Expenditure and Savings and subtract that figure from your Total Income. What is the difference?

8 Are you satisfied with the result? Well done! If not, decide what you can do differently to ensure that you are in control of your money. (Should you save more? Could you cut down on items you do not really need? Should you save before you buy anything, instead of borrowing money? Do you use money for enjoyment, while being responsible? In other words, do you use money in a balanced way?)

Tip: It is a good financial principle to save 10 per cent of your income before you spend the rest of your money. Savings should be put aside before anything else.

The first Law of Money: people first, then money, then things.

Suze Orman (1999)

Guidelines: Activity Sheet 9

My monthly budget

Learning points

Taking financial responsibility, even in big companies, requires certain basic budgeting skills. The same principles necessary for personal finances are applied in business.

Comments

1 Read through the table on Activity Sheet 9 with the group, clarifying uncertainties.
2 Instruct the children to complete their personal lists, consulting with learning partners should they feel they could benefit from it.
3 Be on stand-by for assistance
4 Ask the group for feedback: 'What have you noticed about your finances and the way you think about them?'

Tip

If you could find an example of a company budget or school budget, it could be used to show to the group what it looks like in reality, how complex it could be, and how accurate it has be, and how careful decision makers have to handle it.

Use newspaper clippings of financial mismanagement, embezzlements and bankruptcies.

Timing

10–15 minutes introduction and sharing information

10 minutes completion

10 minutes feedback and summary

9 My monthly budget

👤👤👤 Individual activity with small group discussions

Today's date:	
Income:	**Amount**
Pocket money	
Extra income earned by myself	
Total income	
Savings	

Expenditure	Amount	
Items		**Needed or Wanted**
Example: Magazines	£4	W (for Wanted)
Total Expenditure		

Total Income	
Savings + Expenditure	
Balance	

Guidelines: Activity Sheet 10

Build a financial future

Learning points

Financial planning for the future is more meaningful when it contributes towards an inspiring personal vision. It becomes easier to stay motivated and to persevere when you remind yourself of your dream.

Comments

1 Point out the importance of respecting other people's dreams and personal goals.
2 Prepare the children by talking about the importance and joy of having a great dream. Share stories of people who succeeded because they kept reminding themselves of their dreams. Think of the well-quoted 'I have a dream...' of Martin Luther King.
3 Children are encouraged to think about themselves as young adults, possibly in a relationship with a significant other, possibly married, possibly with children.
4 At the end of the activity, ask the children what they have learnt about themselves, their ambitions and the dreams of their friends/learning partners.
5 Conclude the session by pointing out the relevance of money in the realization of the dreams.
6 Stress the importance of personal happiness and good, supportive relationships and having fun while working towards a meaningful goal.
7 The last question is related to an anchor (an object, picture, gesture, sound, smell or word that reminds you of your dreams or a decision). In this case the anchor should be placed where it could be accessed often. For instance if it is a picture, it could be placed in a very visible spot in the person's room.
8 If considered appropriate, each child could share with the large group what they would use as an anchor and why they made the choice.

Timing

10 minutes introducing the topic

20 minutes drawing and sharing in small groups

5 minutes conclusion with final remarks from the teacher

10 Build a financial future

♟ On your own

Draw a picture of your life when you will be 30 years old.

How are you going to keep on reminding yourself of your financial goals? (Consider using a picture, an object, a note somewhere in your room, etc.)

Guidelines: Activity Sheet 11

Being an entrepreneur

Learning points

Not all people are born entrepreneurs, and certainly many will never need to be entrepreneurs, but when you adopt the entrepreneurial mindset, you consider productivity and adding value seriously. Even employees in regular jobs could benefit from such an approach.

The activity:

- clarifies the concept of self-sufficiency through self-employment and thinking independently.
- encourages children to talk to business people.
- leads children to do research on possible career choices and entrepreneurial alternatives.
- teaches children to find help, how to look for help and how to ask for it.

The knowledge and skills addressed in this activity help build resilience.

Comments

1 Lead the discussion on admirable business people by referring to well-known entrepreneurs, and paying attention to the personal attributes of these entrepreneurs. (Think of Richard Branson, Bill Gates and others.)
2 The children report back on real-life talks or interviews with people in their community, and some information regarding their own preferences regarding a career or business.
3 They could gather information about qualifications, challenges, rewards, etc. and present it to the larger group.

Timing

3 minutes introduction and discussion of well-known entrepreneurs

3 minutes discussion of the questions in the first part of the activity sheet

5 minutes advising where to find information for the poster and related research work

45 minutes preparing the poster in the classroom, unless given as home activity

20 minutes feedback on individual posters with the emphasis on pointing out the best aspects in each child's end product, and learning something from each child's poster

2 minutes closure

11 Being an entrepreneur

Should you want to change jobs one day, or lose your job, how will you handle the situation? How will you be able to carry on with your life? Discuss the importance of:

● money in the bank

● useful skills

● a business of your own.

Prepare a poster for presentation to the larger group, with important elements of your dream job or career. You may make your own drawings, or you could use magazine clippings.

Tips

It may be helpful to talk to business people you know, people in careers that you are interested in, and friends of people in business. You could also find information on the internet, in magazines, in newspapers and other sources.

Imagine someone offers you the opportunity to meet informally with a business person you truly admire, and you will be given 10 minutes with the person. You are instructed to ask only three questions of the person. Which three questions would you ask them? Formulate the questions in the box below. Prepare to share your questions with the large group.

Consider the following requirements for the job, career or business, and make it part of your presentation:

● qualifications

● experience

● challenges

● enjoyable parts of the job

● environment in which you will probably work

● your personal attributes fitting the job, career or business.

12 *Action plan*

👤 On your own

Use the list below to help you plan your future actions. What would you like to do more of? There is space at the end for you to add your own items.

Item

1	Remind myself that I can make money work for me	☐
2	Work according to a budget	☐
3	Keep a record of how I spend my money	☐
4	Save a part of my pocket money	☐
5	Make money by selling something	☐
6	Put money aside for something special	☐
7	Talk to someone who knows how to start a small business	☐
8	Encourage my family to talk about money matters	☐
9	Find someone that will support me with my plans	☐
10	Remind myself regularly of my dreams	☐
11	Make sure that I also sometimes enjoy my money	☐
12	Celebrate when I have saved enough for a special item	☐
13	Remember to give some of my money to a worthwhile cause	☐
14	Find inexpensive ways to enjoy myself	☐
15	Say 'no' when necessary	☐
16	Encourage others to use their money wisely	☐
17	Avoid buying things on impulse	☐
18	Research different types of business by talking to people	☐
19		
20		

What will others notice about your behaviour, which will be proof of your decision to make the most of your money matters?

Diversity

We work together

Outline

Outcomes

On completion of this unit, children should have the knowledge, skills and attitudes to:

- name the things that make us different.

- describe facets of their own culture.

- recognize differences between cultures.

- notice unique characteristics of their own culture.

- understand why it is important to respect other cultures.

- know what a natural resource is.

- appreciate the diversity of natural resources.

- be proud of the things their country has preserved through generations.

- be careful with non-renewable resources – the things that cannot be replaced or made by human beings.

- name products imported from other countries.

- discuss how we could be influenced by damage to the natural environment.

- explain why it is necessary for all countries to use shared resources with good judgement and care.

- suggest how we can protect places of special value.

- know which places are sensitive and require extra care.

> When you handle yourself, use your head; when you handle others,
> use your heart.
>
> *Donna Reed*

Overview

A global perspective

Flexible thinking and mutual acceptance are particularly relevant in today's world. Our differences seem to be more in the foreground than our similarities, judged by our ability to maintain peaceful global relationships. Countries all over the globe experience the results of unresolved differences in other parts of the world. Our quality of life could be affected significantly by decisions taken elsewhere in the world, and in some respects our very existence might depend on some of those decisions.

As the world becomes smaller through mass communication and modern technology, we do more business on a global scale. Our thinking (and feelings!) should be flexible enough to bridge vast differences in culture, as we choose to work across cultural boundaries.

The general workforce increasingly becomes more diverse, challenging our adaptability on a daily basis. Groups previously labelled 'minorities' now rank as 'majorities'. We have to adapt our strategies in managing and developing human resources.

Even within the same company employees often complain that they work in functional 'chimneys'. It means that employees from different departments find it difficult to understand each other's needs and seldom have the time to talk to one another. Therefore they do not know how to support each other in the best possible way in order to create a cohesive company. Ideally, all people in one organization should work together to deliver the best service to customers through effective cross-functional processes.

In schools, children are the customers. As internal customers, they need a well-structured organization that runs smoothly in order to benefit optimally from their education. With the pressures of being a teacher in today's society, this ideal poses quite a challenge. Especially when teachers need to cope with children's behavioural problems that hamper teaching and learning. It is during the early stages of development that children need to acquire the principles of respect, tolerance and positive contribution within a group

context. The behavioural skills that are lacking are not purely academic, but rather of an emotional (personal and interpersonal) nature. In the long run, a combination of academic and emotional skills forms a good starting point for healthy global business participation.

Sharing international resources

> Irrational barriers and ancient prejudices fall quickly when the question of survival itself is at stake.
>
> *John F. Kennedy*

All of us living on this planet share resources. We need to manage our shared global resources in a comprehensive, responsible way. With many natural resources under threat, successful international negotiations will require cultural sensitivity, especially since resources are more than products and monetary funds. It includes human resources with cultural differences!

By learning to understand each other on a personal basis, and accepting differences as an inherent part of being alive, we could lay the basis for healthier future co-operation between countries and regions. It starts with the beliefs, values and attitudes of the individuals that form the global system.

We could help children to understand and appreciate themselves and their culture. Respect for others is based on our respect for ourselves – who we are and the things that made us the kind of people we have become. Our beliefs, values and principles determine our attitudes and behaviour towards others. This unit aims to promote an appreciation of differences, with a definite effort to find similarities on which to build lasting productive relationships and understanding.

For meaningful co-operation, citizens will need useful skills – including the skills to work with others. By valuing diversity, individuals and nations could find ways to work together to the benefit of all.

In the coming century there will be no national products or technologies, no national corporations, no national industries. There will no longer be national economies… All that will remain, rooted within national borders, are the people who comprise a nation. Each nation's primary assets will be its citizens' skills.

Robert Reich (1991)

Linking cultural diversity and resilience

Highly resilient individuals are flexible thinkers and are therefore comfortable with cultural differences, yet have a strong sense of their own identity. For that reason the development of resilient learners needs to include the personal and interpersonal skills necessary for making the most of differences in a diverse society.

As future workers, parents and decision makers, children will have to find their way in a much wider, more complex society than that of their parents. To develop citizens that are assets to their country, the process of balancing personal identity with society's needs should ideally start early in life. The earlier we start the process, the more effective our efforts will be.

Guidelines
and
Activity Sheets

Guidelines: Activity Sheet 1

My place in the world

Learning points

Where we come from and where we currently stay affects our reality and lifestyle. However, humankind is an interrelated system in which we all need to understand how we influence each other, need each other and can contribute to each other. International trade necessitates that we learn to work together.

Comments

1 The first part of this activity (steps 1–3) addresses geographical location. The children need to find their country on the map and colour it in. With eyes closed, they then make a mark at random. This is the starting point for a discussion on how a specific region influences lifestyle.

2 The second part of the activity (step 4) is to ask the children to think about the most beautiful place they have ever been to, or seen in pictures or on TV. Let them describe the places to each other in small groups.

Tip

The use of newspaper clippings on oil price increases, the effects of war, food shortages, boycotts, etc. could be used to show the links between nations. A large map of the world in the form of a wall chart or good atlas will be really helpful during this activity.

Resources

A large map or atlas, or book on regional geography, could be used in a group context to locate countries and products. The use of posters and films about beautiful places in different parts of the world could also add to the frame of reference.

Timing

2 minutes introductory talk

10 minutes to locate and colour country and complete discussion

20 minutes to locate regions and products

5 minutes discussing questions 6, 7 and 8 as a large group

2 minutes conclusion

1 *My place in the world*

👤👤👤 Small group discussion

1 Study the map of the world. Colour the area on the map that represents your country. What do you notice about the position and size of your country when you compare it to others?

2 Close your eyes and make a dot on the map on your activity sheet. What is the area called where you placed your dot?

3 How would your life be different if you were living in the area where you put the dot? (If it was in the sea, what would your life on a ship be like?)

4 Think of the most beautiful place you have ever been to (or that you have seen on TV, in a movie or in a picture). What made the place special? Describe the place. How would it make you feel if you knew that you would never be allowed to see the place again because it does not exist anymore?

5 Different products are produced or found in different places in the world. Use your map to find the location of as many of the items on the list below as you can (there may be more than one location for each item on the list) or challenge another learning group to see who can find the most locations – see who can do this in the shortest time span.

> Tea
>
> Sugar
>
> Oats
>
> Cotton
>
> Rich deposits of iron
>
> Gold
>
> Diamonds
>
> Oil
>
> Natural gas
>
> Abundance of fish
>
> Natural forests
>
> Citrus fruit such as oranges
>
> Cattle for milk, meat and leather
>
> Sheep

As a group, you could also look for additional international products, manufacturers, or places of interest.

6 What would happen if countries did not trade their products?

7 List ten products that would not be available in your local supermarket, if international trade did not happen?

8 What happens if countries find it impossible to share information, products and good relationships?

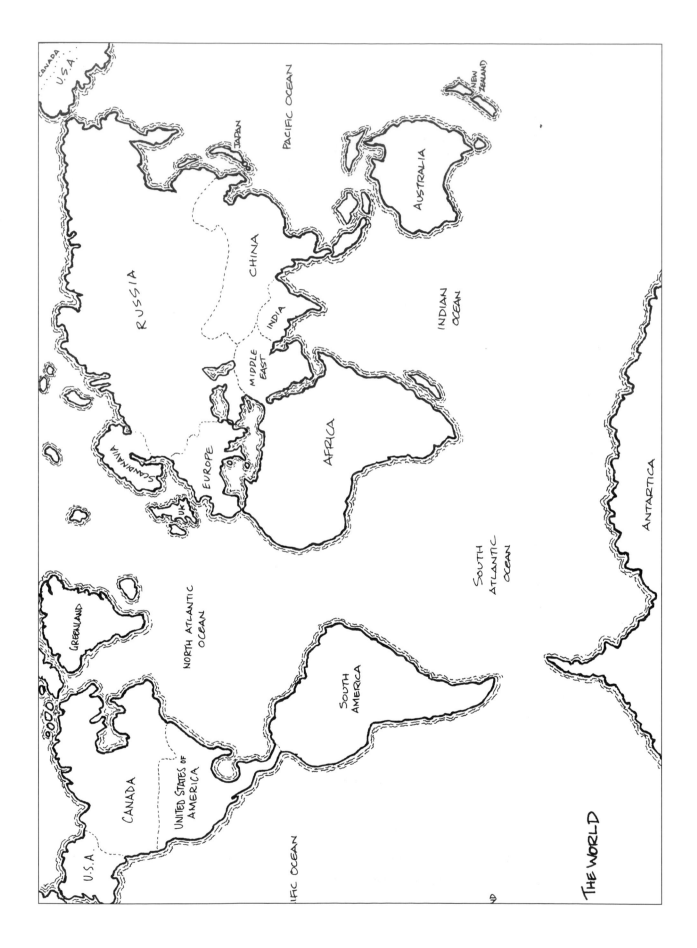

Guidelines: Activity Sheet 2

Cultural awareness

Learning points

Habits and etiquette are not universal and to learn about other cultures can be fascinating and enriching. We can also adopt useful habits from others. This activity aims to stimulate awareness and sensitivity to other people's (or culture's) frames of reference, their needs and preferences.

Comments

The children complete the questionnaire in groups of three to five. At the end of the activity they put forward their opinions in the larger group, while the teacher offers the 'correct' answers (see below and page 154) and guides the discussion. It is possible that children from different cultures could add to the information, or even have different bits of information. The idea is not to be rigid, but accept that even in a specific culture there could be variations and different interpretations.

Tip

The more diverse the discussion groups, the more interesting the discussion will be.

Timing

1 minute introduction

5–10 minutes small group discussions

15 minutes sharing interesting information

1 minute conclusion

Cultural awareness questionnaire
Answer sheet

1 Is it polite for individuals all over the world to look others directly in the eye?

   In many Western countries, it is considered proper to look into a person's eyes, but not for longer than a second. In Asia, Japan and Africa, people may look down instead of making eye contact when they want to show respect.

2 Is it acceptable everywhere to give people compliments in front of others?

   No. Asian-born individuals may prefer not to be praised in front of everyone. In Japan the following guidelines apply:
   - Be punctual
   - Do not maintain direct eye contact
   - Do not touch anybody
   - Handshaking is not widely used as a greeting
   - Bow only if someone bows to you
   - Keep your voice and gestures subdued
   - Shoes are not removed at places of business but be prepared to remove your shoes at restaurants and homes
   - Gifts are expected but are not opened in front of the giver.

3 Would all Asian-born individuals openly complain when they are unhappy with something?

   No. Many would rather stay quiet because it is considered bad manners to upset others in public.

---

4 Does the 'OK' gesture made with the fingers and thumb forming a circle mean the same throughout the world?

No. In Spanish-speaking countries and Greece it is a very rude sign. Do not point a finger or beckon another person closer with a crooked finger in Japan and Indonesia.

5 Would a Chinese person really appreciate a grandfather's clock as a present?

No. Giving a clock as a gift is considered to bring bad luck to the person receiving it.

More information on Chinese customs:

● Do not make any body contact – no hugs, kisses or touching

● Use a quiet voice and demeanour

● The family name comes first – Mr Fung Lee is Mr Fung

● Learn to enjoy tea – it will be served often

● Dress very conservatively – do not wear white

● Rather than displease you with the truth, the Chinese will avoid it.

6 Do people all over Europe greet each other by shaking hands once?

No. Italians, Romanians or Czechoslovakians may shake the hand up and down seven times each time they greet a person. In Japan, handshaking is not common as a greeting. In Portugal, Spain and Latin America men embrace or hug in greeting.

7 In Arab countries is alcohol a welcome gift?

No. Alcohol is not acceptable on religious grounds. Alcohol is not allowed into Saudi Arabia.

8 In Arab countries is it an insult to refuse food or drink when offered by a host or hostess?

Yes. Offering and accepting food and drink is seen as hospitality and good manners.

More information:

● Food and drink is often offered before business – eat what you can, even if you are not hungry

● Wear a light-weight dark suit, shirt and tie – no trousers or shorts for women

● Use you right hand – the left hand is used for very personal hygiene

● Do not point at or beckon a person

● Arabs stand very close in conversation – do not step back

● Do not enquire about an Arab's family – private life is not discussed

● Keep your feet on the floor – do not expose the soles of your feet

● Do not tease, argue or in any way hurt your host's pride.

9 When doing business in Africa, one should not be in a hurry. True or false?

True. Africans prefer to take their time when conducting business. In Mexico, Egypt and Ethiopia being late is not considered rude.

10 In every country is 'yes' and 'no' indicated by moving the head from side to side or up and down.

No. In some countries, like Bulgaria, it means the opposite.

2 Cultural awareness questionnaire

♟♟♟ Small group

In a group of four or five, answer the following questions. Be prepared to give feedback to the larger group. You may make notes in the spaces on the table.

Cultural awareness questionnaire

1 Is it polite for individuals all over the world to look others directly in the eye?

2 Is it acceptable everywhere to give people compliments in front of others?

3 Would all Asian-born individuals openly complain when they are unhappy with something?

4 Does the 'OK' gesture made with the fingers and thumb forming a circle mean the same throughout the world?

5 Would a Chinese person really appreciate a grandfather's clock as a present?

6 Do people all over Europe greet each other by shaking hands once?

7 In Arab countries is alcohol a welcome gift?

8 In Arab countries is it an insult to refuse food or drink when offered by a host or hostess?

9 When doing business in Africa, one should not be in a hurry. True or false?

10 In every country is 'yes' and 'no' indicated by moving the head from side to side or up and down?

Guidelines: Activity Sheet 3

A cultural quiz

Learning points

This activity allows children to assess their flexibility of thought and openness to new experiences.

Comments

1 The teacher reads through the questions and allows a few moments for self-assessment.
2 The children tick the statements they can identify with.

Timing

10 minutes discussion

3 A cultural quiz

👤 On your own

Read the questions below. For every question that you can answer 'yes', put a tick in the box on the right.

Your opinion	Tick
1 Are there any beautiful places elsewhere in the world that you would like to visit?	☐
2 Do you have friends from different cultures and ethnic groups?	☐
3 Apart from your home language, will you learn to speak at least one foreign language?	☐
4 When you hear music, can you tell from which part of the world it comes by the sounds and instruments used?	☐
5 Can you explain the basic rules of any sport or games that are not typical of your country?	☐
6 There are friendly people all over the world – in each country will there be helpful, friendly people?	☐
7 Do you think you would be comfortable to live or work in another country when you are an adult?	☐
8 Do you have friends from different types of households?	☐
9 Do you enjoy trying out different types of food and even eating foods that some people consider 'weird' or unusual?	☐
10 Do you know about the culture of quite a few other countries because you have read about them or watched television programmes on them?	☐

The more ticks you have made, the more comfortable you are with variety and cultural differences. This questionnaire is a tool to help you think about differences and the way we deal with them. There are many more ways in which we are different, and our challenge is to find ways to work together despite differences.

Guidelines: Activity Sheet 4

Democracy

Learning points

Sometimes we have to make decisions as a large group, such as when the people of a country elect new leaders, or when a large group of people decide on the future of an area. During such time, as an individual you have to accept the outcome of the majority decision whether you like it or not.

Comments

1 Place ten large pictures of a variety of themes on the board. Alternatively you could print ten quotes on paper and display them to the group.
2 The pictures or quotes could be pasted on a board if you prefer.
3 The children then need to work in groups of five or six. Each group has to stand together and quietly make decisions so that other groups do not hear what they decide. As a small group they vote for a favourite picture or quote with which the group can identify.
4 The rules are:
   ● Once the group has made the decision, no further discussion will be allowed and opinions cannot be changed.
   ● The vote is the final answer.
5 The small groups elect a speaker on behalf of the group, who explains to the larger group why they have selected the picture or quote of their choice.
6 Individual children are invited to share how they feel about letting go of their personal preferences in favour of democracy.
7 Ask the smaller groups how they elected their spokesperson or speaker.
8 Relate the process to democracy and how leaders are chosen.
9 Discuss the importance of co-operation once a decision has been taken, even if you do not agree.
10 Ask: 'When is it acceptable to object, and when is it necessary to form a pressure group to change a decision or existing practice?'
11 Conclude and summarize.

Timing

2 minutes giving instructions, clarifying the rules of the game and organizing groups

5 minutes for small group activities

10 minutes individual feedback in the large group about personal experiences during the exercise and general comments about the process of making democratic decisions.

5 minutes general discussion in the large group

2 minutes closure

4 Democracy

👥👥👥 Small group

Sometimes we have to make decisions as a large group, such as when the people of a country elect new leaders, or when a large group of people decide on the future of an area.

1 Work in groups of five or six. Stand or sit together and as quietly as possible take your decision. As a small group, vote for a favourite picture or quote with which you can all identify.

2 The rules are:

● Once the group has made the decision, no further discussion will be allowed, and opinions cannot be changed.

● The vote is the final answer.

3 Elect a speaker on behalf of your group, who will explain to the larger group why you have chosen the specific picture or quote.

4 How did you choose your leader?

5 Why is it important to give your co-operation once a decision has been taken, even if you do not agree?

6 When is it acceptable to object or disagree with a democratic decision?

7 When is it necessary to form a pressure group to change something in your community or country?

8 How are the leaders in our country chosen?

9 Are all the citizens happy with the leaders of the country?

10 Do you know how laws are made in this country?

11 Why are laws made in the first place?

12 If someone breaks the law, and you know it, how does it make you feel?

13 What should you do if you see or know that someone is breaking the law?

Guidelines: Activity Sheet 5

Our world

Learning points

Each person has a unique perspective and appreciation for the world we live in. Children have their hopes and dreams for the environment they will eventually utilize and manage. This activity stimulates thoughts on what they want, as opposed to what they fear or do not want.

Comments

Each child creates a drawing on Activity Sheet 5 of an element of what that child would like to be part of in an ideal world. This could be peace, excitement, friendship, a beautiful place, etc. When everybody has completed their drawing, the drawings are cut out and combined in a large mosaic that is glued together, sealed or framed and put up for display. This could form part of the class decorations, or could even be positioned in a central place in the school for display.

Tip

Show the group examples of collages or mosaics, using pictures. An inspiring video could also be shown.

Timing

25 minutes per drawing

20 minutes for assembling

5 *Our world*

👤 On your own

Make a drawing of something you would really love to have as part of the world. What would give you great satisfaction if it existed or kept on being there for you to enjoy?

Think of peace, happiness, beautiful places, health, friendship or anything that will have meaning for you.

Draw your picture in the square below but make sure it fits into the space because the square will be used as part of a collage. Each person in the class will have a drawing in the combined picture that the group will put together at the end of the session.

6 *Action plan*

👤 On your own

To make a difference in my world, I will always…
Next time I see a person from another country I will…
Every time I travel in my own country I will…
What I love most about my country is…
When I hear another person say something hurtful about a person from another race or colour I will…
If I learn a new language, it will be…
The exotic (foreign, unknown) food that I would like to try is…
One day I am going to help protect the environment by…
Own decision:

Moving on

Adapting, hoping and growing

Outline

Outcomes

On completion of this unit, children should have the necessary knowledge, skills and attitudes to reflect on how to deal with change. To deal with change in the most effective way, they should be able to:

- enjoy learning new things (love learning).

- prepare for the change as well as they can.

- change because they want to move on.

- understand that change is not always easy.

- make peace with uncertainties.

- believe that things will work out.

- accept that being scared of the unknown is natural.

- find ways to cope with their emotions.

- be open for new opportunities.

- make difficult situations easier by addressing issues step by step.

- understand that new opportunities are going to open up.

- talk about personal dilemmas and ambiguity.

Welcome to tomorrow when computers aren't the only things that will get smarter. You will too.

Dryden and Vos (1994)

Overview

The world of work is changing. Old ways of doing things are being replaced, improved, sometimes destroyed and cast aside as the world moves on. Products emerge and disappear; brands are promoted and eradicated; legendary names bite the corporate dust. The way we make things is being revolutionized. The way we buy and consume products is undergoing a transformation. The way we manage is being shaken like a cocktail. The list is endless and affects the fundamentals we once took for granted –
the way we work,
the way we play,
the way we live our lives.

White et al. (1996)

Many people believe that the school system is twenty years behind the times in developing skills and behaviours for the rapidly changing world of work.

Changes happen so fast that there is a constant need to adapt your way of thinking, communicating, decision making and even life style. Careers emerge and vanish depending on new developments. All this has a great impact on career options and preparation for the future.

Children going from primary school to secondary school might look forward to this move. Some might have their doubts about the new environment. Most of them will be apprehensive, whether they are showing it or not. Whatever their expectations are, it is important that they think about the future and prepare themselves to make the most of the opportunities.

In secondary school, children need to select subjects with their future career in mind. Subject choices ideally need to open up career opportunities. Even at this age the subject choices are about working with people, figures or things.

These decisions can be daunting. Some children may question their abilities to make a success of their dream careers, while even more children do not know what they would like to be in the future. Although you have to accept the principle of lifelong learning, it really makes things easier if you have a good start.

It is during this transition stage that children need good self-esteem to cope with the challenges. They also need to know themselves in order to choose the right subjects for the right careers. To really know themselves is, however, a tall order.

Potential challenges in primary school	Potential challenges in adolescence
● Beginning another school year	● Breaking up with a boyfriend or girlfriend
● An outstanding personal achievement	● Becoming involved with drugs or alcohol
● Beginning school	● Increase in number of arguments with parents
● Moving to a new school district	● Beginning secondary school
● An increase in number of arguments with parents	● Beginning to date
● Death of a grandparent	● Outstanding personal achievements
● Mother beginning to work	● Not being accepted for an extracurricular activity
● Serious illness of a parent requiring hospitalization	● Death of a close friend
● Change in parents' financial status	● Change in parents' financial status
● Brother or sister leaving home	● Brother or sister leaving home
● Divorce of parents	● Dealing with growing sexuality
● Developing intellectual competence	● Changes in body image during puberty
	● Selecting a career
	● Coping with independence
	● Leaving home for study purpose or the armed forces
	● Success in school-leaving examinations

Adapted from Masuda and Holmes (1978)

Order	Resistance	Chaos	Creativity	Order
Comfort and routine	Expect discomfort	Depressed and lonely	Experience great pain	Learn what works
Control	Chaos	Nothing works	Try new things	See patterns
Grumble	Blame	Despair	Energy	Focus

Life events and possible impact

From the table on page 166 you could make deductions about the challenges that children are potentially dealing with and how it could assist parents and teachers to support them in processing life events.

The process of change

There are various models and theories about the effects of change and transition on people. Some models are specifically designed for organizational change, yet offer useful insights in terms of what individuals go through. The adapted five phase model above, originally developed by Renate Volpe (2000), is such an example.

In reality, change happens constantly and you could have stability in one area of your life while you undergo change in other areas. It is when you simultaneously experience change in various areas of your life that the combined impact could be damaging – it is the last snowflake that causes the avalanche.

Some changes are more traumatic than others; for instance, when you lose a loved one, it is normally more traumatic than changing jobs or getting a promotion. Depending on where you are in terms of change and adaptation, you might experience the following:

Your primary reaction	Thinking, feeling and doing
1 What is happening?	Think: Surprise, detached Feel: Dull, numb, paralysed Do: Freeze, stay inactive
2 I don't believe it!	Think: Disbelief, confused Feel: Fear, loneliness Do: Nothing
3 What am I to do?	Think: Sceptical, indecisive Feel: Confused, grieving, uncertain Do: Resist action
4 I resent this!	Think: Bitter, agitated Feel: Angry, guilty, resentful Do: Isolate self from others
5 I accept it.	Think: Acceptance Feel: Resigned, at peace Do: New energy and purpose

6 What is the meaning of this?	Think: Objective, analytical Feel: Thankful, hopeful and excited Do: Plan ahead
7 I have made it!	Think: Insight and appreciation Feel: Centred, satisfied and connected Do: Act leniently and with tolerance
8 I am moving on.	Think: Creative, optimistic Feel: Self-assured and confident Do: Act competently, focused
9 What? A new challenge?	Think: Confused yet searching Feel: Uncentred yet competent Do: Reflect and visualize

Not everybody reacts in exactly the same way, but if you know what could potentially be part of a child's experience, it might help you to guide and assist more effectively.

> The only limit to our realization of tomorrow will be our doubts of today.
>
> *Franklin D. Roosevelt*

Experiences that build resilience

Children build resilience when they experience the following:

1 *Competence: feeling capable and successful*
   When children are entrusted with specific responsibilities and tasks, the acknowledgement of even the smallest of tasks and behaviours that are successfully accomplished can foster the experience of competence.

2 *Optimism: feeling encouraged and hopeful*
   Resilient learners have high expectations for the future, and you can reinforce those expectations with praise and encouragement.

3 *Potency: feeling empowered*
   You are empowered when you have applicable knowledge and useful skills. For 'whole person empowerment', competencies should ideally include academic skills as well as personal,

interpersonal and social skills. Even those who are not academically strong can be successful in life when they know how to make the most of their personalities and talents and their relationships with others.

4 *Usefulness: feeling needed*
   When you are able to do things for other people that make their lives easier and when they ask you to do favours or help with chores, it makes you feel needed. This, however, is not the same as getting boring tasks dumped on you.

5 *Belonging: feeling valued*
   To feel part of a group, loved, accepted and respected are social needs. You feel valued when you get the opportunity to be heard within a group, and when your opinion is respected and acknowledged.

Adapted from Pikes *et al.* (1998)

Many of the emotions described above could be enhanced through positive feedback from people that children respect and trust. It helps to give positive feedback even on very basic skills, especially if a child is challenged with normal school work. In large group discussions it is particularly valuable to give acknowledgement to those with the need for encouragement.

When children feel good about themselves, they handle change better.

Using affirmations to build resilience

An affirmation is a positive thought that you deliberately choose to put into your mind. You might think of affirmations as positive thinking or positive self-talk. Affirmations are reminders to yourself that although you may not have control over people, situations and events in your life, you do have control over your reactions to such things. You can choose your attitudes and actions.

Effective affirmations:

- begin with 'I' (your name).
- are stated in the present tense.
- use positive, active verbs to empower your affirmation with feelings (not what you will not do or do not want).
- are phrased as if the desired results were already present.
- are repeated every day.

For example: 'I am able to find all the resources I need to successfully... (name what you want to achieve).'

Therefore:

- With an affirmation you affirm in the present something you want in your future.
- You are today what you thought you were yesterday!
- If you think you can or if you think you can't, you're right!

Today we realize that when we change our inner minds (our beliefs and attitudes), it automatically leads to change in the external aspects of our lives.

Where there is genuine vision, people excel and learn, not because they are told to, but because they want to.

Peter M. Senge (1992)

The courage to move on

Change can happen gradually, or it can be an unexpected surprise. Sometimes change is your personal choice, like changing subjects, deciding to end a friendship or beginning a new relationship, or attending a new school. Other changes are the result of external factors like a natural disaster, a government decision, a war or a company bankruptcy. Whether the change process is something you brought on yourself or not, the process holds uncertainties and probably an unexpected turn of events. This could lead to fear for the unknown. The fear and stressful emotions could paralyse you and hamper your decision making and pro-activity. But, you simply have to move on.

Courage is not the absence of fear; rather it is the ability to take action in the face of fear.

Nancy Anderson (1994)

80% of learning difficulties are related to stress. Remove the stress and you remove the difficulties.

Gordon Stokes, President, Three in One Concepts (quoted in Dryden and Vos, 1994)

And when you move on, despite stress, fear and doubts the end result could be unexpectedly positive. Even if it does not work out exactly the way you planned, it offers you different opportunities and new beginnings.

We are not here just to survive and live long. We are here to live and know life in its multi-dimensions, to know life in its richness, in all its variety. And when a man lives multi-dimensionally, explores all possibilities available, never shrinks back from any challenge, but rushes to welcome it and rises to the occasion, then life becomes a flame; life blooms.

Bhagwan Shree Rajneesh (quoted in Volpe, 2000)

Guidelines
and
Activity Sheets

Guidelines: Activity Sheet 1

Motivation

Learning points

Motivation could be based on fear or internal motivation – being controlled from within (internal locus of control) or from outside (external locus of control). When you know what you want, you find the energy and time to move and take action.

Comments

1 Discuss the idea of fear versus being excited about something.
2 Read through the self-assessment questionnaire and clarify any uncertainties.
3 Be on standby to assist with the questionnaire.
4 Ask the children what they have learnt.
5 Summarize and conclude.

Tip

Ask the children how it feels to fear something or somebody, and how it feels to do something based on fear. Refer to the experience of creativity and joy when you do things you enjoy and want to do.

Timing

10 minutes introduction and discussion of fear, inspiration, etc.

10 minutes self-assessment and feedback

5 minutes concluding

1 *Motivation*

👤 On your own

Are you moved by a carrot or by a stick? Being motivated by a carrot means that you do things because you want to, for your own reasons. It is fulfilling your dreams and wishes and almost feels like you are being pulled towards your dreams.

If you need a stick to get you moving, you are driven by fear. This is a force away from something bad or negative that you don't want. However, fear is not always enough to get you on track to something worthwhile. You first need to know what you want. Many people say: 'I know what I do not want, but I don't know what I do want!' This is not good news for moving on with confidence and peace of mind.

How motivated are you? What is pulling you? Tick the remarks that are true for you on the questionnaire below.

Dreams

1	I have dreams for the future	☐
2	I know what I want	☐

Self-motivation

3	I do what I have to do, without someone watching me	☐
4	I work on my own to achieve my own goals	☐

Positive mindset

5	I am excited about my future one day	☐
6	I look forward to next year	☐

Inquisitive mindset

7	New places interest me	☐
8	I am interested in new subjects and information	☐

Self-esteem

9	I know I can make a success of my life	☐
10	I know that I will be able to make new friends	☐

Ownership

11	When moving on to something new, I plan and prepare for it	☐
12	When I feel uncertain, I find out what I can from others	☐

Self-management

13	I decide how I react to things happening to me	☐
14	I determine how I experience new things	☐

More ticks mean that you are willing and prepared to move on to new challenges.

Guidelines: Activity Sheet 2

Moving on or losing out?

Learning points

Change can be painful and scary, unless you deal with it in a productive way. There will probably always be an element of fear when you deal with the unknown. The challenge is to manage fear to a level that is productive and allows for high-energy inputs instead of going into survival mode or reflex. Gathering information, visiting a new place (school), planning what you are going to do, talking with others already familiar with the place, meeting people enrolled in the new school, etc. could help. In short, being pro-active helps.

Comments

1 Use Activity Sheet 2 to guide discussions in pairs.
2 Explain what the categories stand for.
3 The children work on their own. On completion, feedback is given to the larger group.

Tip

Have a short discussion on fear of the unknown and how it is normal and healthy if addressed and managed well.

Timing

5 minutes introduction

10 minutes working in pairs

5 minutes concluding

2 Moving on or losing out?

👥 Share in pairs

When you have to move on, you leave some things behind, and new experiences await you. When you think of next year, how does it make you feel?

With a learning partner, add to the four lists below:

What can I lose?	What can I gain?
Examples: Good friends Favourite teacher	*Example:* New friends
How can I make things more difficult?	**How can I make things easier?**
Examples: Pretending it is not going to happen Refusing to talk about it Talking only about it Not crying	*Examples:* Talk to a friend Ask for help

Guidelines: Activity Sheet 3

My body of support

Learning points

Resilient individuals know how to contract help. When you have a support system, you feel secure and experience social connection and cohesion (feeling close to people and feeling part of a group). This is also the basis of a strong society that makes people feel safe, protected and supported.

Comments

1 Do a brief overview of how people need each other for support.
2 Instruct the children to complete the self-assessment on Activity Sheet 3. They may find assistance from learning partners very useful.
3 Guide a general discussion on mutual caring and assistance.
4 Conclude.

Tip

Refer to the principles of people being dependent on others and therefore having a life purpose implies that you know what you can do well to make a difference to other people's lives. You also need to allow others to help you. This need of people to help others and to ask for help is part of being interdependent, yet self-sufficient.

Timing

5 minutes overview

12 minutes self-assessment

10 minutes general discussion

5 minutes concluding

3 *My body of support*

👤 On your own

You are not alone in this world. There are people who could assist you in some ways. Consider the following questions and write down the names of the people who could help you.

Description of role	Person's name
1 Who gets me to think for myself?	
2 Who challenges me to move on?	
3 Who listens to me when I need an ear?	
4 Who celebrates with me when I complete a task?	
5 Who cheers me when I have success?	
6 Who finds out new opportunities and encourages me to try them out?	
7 Who loves me?	
8 Who consoles me when I am sad?	
9 Who brings fun into my life?	
10 Who turns my arguments around and forces me to think differently?	
11 More roles?	
12	
13	
14	

Guidelines: Activity Sheet 4

Fear

Learning points

Chance implies a certain level of fear. Fear in itself is only bad if not managed. Apprehension often ensures that you take extra care and therefore deliver outstanding outputs.

Comments

1 Talk the group through the activity, then allow sharing in pairs.
2 Ask for feedback to the larger group.
3 List learning points on the boards.
4 Conclude.

Tip

Explain that courage is not about having no fear, it is about taking action in the face of fear.

Timing

5 minutes introduction

15–20 minutes sharing in pairs

5 minutes discussion and feedback

2 minutes concluding

4 Fear

False

Evidence

Appearing

Real

👥 Share in pairs

Many of the things we are worried about, never happen. Think of things you have feared in the past that did not happen. List them in the space below.

What do you fear now?

What do you fear right now?

Where do you feel fear?

Can you do something about it?

List five things you could do to get rid of the fear.

1

2

3

4

5

Guidelines: Activity Sheet 5

Excuses?

Learning points

You can put things off indefinitely by coming up with excuses – because you are scared, lazy, unmotivated, etc. whatever the reasons may be. The point is that finding excuses takes effort too, and does not contribute to healthy self-esteem.

Comments

1 Lead a general discussion on the habit of making excuses, and explore where it comes from.
2 The children list their excuses on the activity sheet (or a separate sheet if preferred).
3 The list of excuses is then put on the floor.
4 Invite the children to dance on their excuses. This is symbolic of taking action and overcoming hindrances. It is also a lot of fun.
5 The excuses are then thrown into the dustbin – symbolically forever.
6 The group share their experiences and learning points.
7 Conclude by asking each participant to name one thing that will not be used as an excuse again.

Tip

The physical 'destruction of excuses' as symbolically done in this activity has experiential value and stands for putting an end to something negative on a permanent basis.

Timing

5 minutes introduction

15 minutes activity

10 minutes wrapping up and concluding with learning points and the resolutions of participants

5 *Excuses*

👥👥 Large group discussion

It is sometimes easier to find excuses for not doing something, or not even trying to do something. Some lame excuses include the following:

- I can't do it
- I have tried this before and it did not work then
- It is hard to learn new things
- This is not the right time for me
- I will do it later
- I don't know what to do
- Nobody will notice in any case

👤 On your own

Can you add a few more excuses?

- Now take this page with all the excuses written on it and dance on it until you cannot see your writing anymore.
- Crumple what is left of the paper and throw it in the dustbin.
- Once the excuses are in the dustbin, you will have to find ten reasons why you can succeed and share them with your group.
- As a final activity, your teacher could list all your reasons for success on the board!

Guidelines: Activity Sheet 6

I can!

Learning points

Believing that you *can* is important in doing anything worthwhile. To build self-esteem, it is important to acknowledge what you already do and to acknowledge your successes. You may underestimate the importance of seemingly unimportant tasks, when they could influence your sense of being trustworthy or persistent. Even small acts are a reflection of who and what you are. Small successes progressively build self-confidence.

Comments

1 Introduce the concept of acknowledgement and self-esteem.
2 Instruct the children to complete the list of successes on Activity Sheet 6.
3 Encourage the children to continue the activity for the next two weeks.
4 Regularly remind them of their commitment.
5 After two weeks, ask for feedback.

Tip

Ask the children how comfortable they think most people are in complimenting themselves. Do they know people that pay themselves compliments during conversations?

Timing

5 minutes introduction

10 minutes completing the list

5 minutes discussion and concluding

6 *I can!*

👤 **On your own**

When you go to bed at night and keep on thinking about mistakes you have made during the day, you feel disappointed in yourself and you may loose your self-esteem. Why not remind yourself of all the good things you did throughout the day?

Just before you go to bed at night, write down everything that you have done successfully during the day. Read through the list just before you go to sleep. Do this for two weeks, then notice how you feel about yourself!

Example:

1   I got out of bed in time to finish my morning routine.
2   I finished my homework before I watched TV.

My list of successes:
1
2
3
4
5
6
7
8
9
10

Guidelines: Activity Sheet 7

My future

Learning point

If you acknowledge what energizes and inspires you, and you understand what you appreciate and value, you will look at your future differently and your decisions will be simplified.

Comments

1 Briefly explain the meaning of the four quadrants.
2 Allow the children to share in groups of four or five.
3 Ask for feedback from each child.
4 Ask what was the most important part of the activity for each child.
5 Conclude with a summary.

Tip

This is potentially a high-energy activity. Ensure that the children understand the meaning of the phrases in the four quadrants.

Timing

3 minutes introduction

15–20 minutes discussion

10 minutes feedback and concluding

7 My future

🎎 Small group activity

When you know what you want and what you enjoy in life, it is easier to plan your future.
In small groups, share the following within your group.

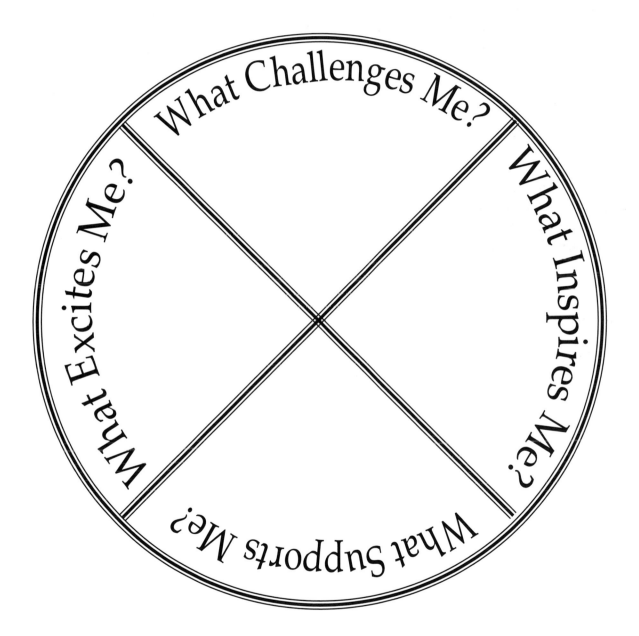

Guidelines: Activity Sheet 8

Becoming a master

Learning points

Mastery is the end result of many things, but so-called masters invariably started to pursue their talents when they were young. Success is a very subjective concept. What makes you successful in your own eyes could be very different from what others consider to be success. However, mastery could be defined more objectively because it is associated with specific skills or results. Not all people want to make the sacrifices and inputs necessary to achieve mastery.

Comments

1   Introduce the topic with a discussion on well-known successful people who started young, or persevered.
2   List the obvious traits or habits of these 'masters'.
3   Talk through the steps in becoming a master, and allow the children to fill in their responses while you work through the different stages on Activity Sheet 8.

Tip

Talk about masters in history, or even today. Think of successful politicians, business people, artists, athletes, etc. Share well-known stories. Use magazine or newspaper articles. Find the elements of what made people achieve mastery.

Timing

10 minutes introduction

15 minutes working through the list, discussing points informally as you go

5 minutes summary and concluding

8 Becoming a master

 On your own

Starting up

In the beginning, you are a 'novice'. You first have to learn the rules of the game. At this stage, you are not sure of how to win the game, you have to concentrate on the steps.

What are you learning to do at the moment?

Improving

As you gain experience, you begin to understand how the game works. You are able to see difficult situations, but you still cannot plan far ahead.

What are you still improving on?

Managing

During this stage you are able to make clever decisions, and plan ahead. You will even be able to explain your game plan to others.

What can you do well enough to manage on your own?

Performing well

You are very good at what you do, and you can do it almost without thinking. You know exactly what is expected from you.

What can you do very well?

Being a master

You can quickly make new plans to win the game. Others learn from you. You only lose the game when you play against another master.

Are you a master, and why do you say so?

What makes you a master?

Learning points

Self-assessment of steps that the individual can control. It is not always the person with the most talent that wins, but the one who does all the right things in the right way at the right time.

Comments

This activity is inspired by Erich Fromm's (1956) four requirements for mastery: Discipline, Patience, Concentration and Supreme Concern.

1 Ask for a few inputs on what makes some people successful. Is it because they have more talent, or is it because they use what they have to the best of their ability?
2 Help children to complete the questionnaire.
3 Ask for general feedback and list learning points.
4 Conclude.

Timing

5 minutes introduction

15 minutes self-assessment and completion of questionnaire

5 minutes concluding

9 *What makes you a master?*

👤 **On your own**

To become a master and be very successful is often more within your reach that you think. There are wonderful stories about people who achieved outstanding success despite all kinds of difficulties, such as competing in the Olympic Games despite a disability (like the well-known athlete Johnson, a sprinter who competed and won in the normal Olympics despite his limp), or playing beautiful music despite being blind. Share stories of such outstanding achievements within the larger group. So what do you need to do to rise above the average?

Complete the questionnaire below by ticking your personal challenges.

Am I disciplined enough?		**Am I patient enough?**	
Do I practise frequently?	☐	Can I wait for results?	☐
Do keep on trying?	☐	Can I go slowly when necessary?	☐
Do I finish what I start?	☐	Do I keep on trying?	☐
Do I plan what I want to do, and stick to the plan?	☐	Do I redo some important things to get them perfect?	☐
Do I know what I am capable of? Is this 'good enough'?	☐	Do I hang on even when I make mistakes or fail?	☐
Can I focus?		**Do I have a clear vision?**	
Do I do only one thing at a time?	☐	Do I know what I am good at?	☐
Can I be alone with myself?	☐	Do I put in effort to be good at what I do?	☐
Can I let go of distracting thoughts?	☐	Do I spend enough time thinking about my dreams?	☐
Do I give it my full attention?	☐	Do I choose my activities to help me achieve my goal?	☐
Do I make the most of this moment?	☐		

Adapted from Erich Fromm (1956)

How can I improve on my way to success and being a master at what I do?

---

10 Action plan

👤 On your own

Tick the statements below that will help you answer the following question.

In order to reach my dream, I will do the following:

Think about my dreams ☐

Say what I want ☐

Try out different things to experience what I am good at ☐

Keep on trying ☐

Ask for help ☐

Find solutions instead of looking for excuses ☐

Help others ☐

Plan ahead ☐

Make sure that I stick to my plans ☐

Celebrate my achievements with people that I care about ☐

Ask for feedback when I need guidance ☐

Get all the information I can to help me decide ☐

Tell myself that I can ☐

Enjoy what I am doing ☐

Find ways to make things easier ☐

Start in time ☐

Remind myself of my goals ☐

Reward myself for things well done ☐

Glossary

Acceptance	To keep on fighting and debating things you cannot change simply depletes your personal resources and can alienate you from others. Acceptance brings inner peace and allows you to focus on important issues.
Accountability	To stand forth and be counted
Achievement	Attaining or earning a goal
Acknowledge	Admit that you have something to do with the situation; indicate that you notice
Adapt	To change in order to adjust to new circumstances
Adversity	Bad luck, hardship
Affirmations	Confirmation of the truth of something; a positive reinforcement of a good attribute
Aggressive people	People who force others to comply with their personal rights, desires, feelings and beliefs, at the cost of the others
Alexthymia	Emotional numbness – not feeling at all
Analytical thinking	Taking apart the elements of a situation and evaluating your effect on the situation
Apologizing	Asking forgiveness or expressing regret
Assertive people	People who stand up for their rights, needs, desires and beliefs
Assertiveness	Calmly and consistently standing up for my rights, without losing my temper or giving up my rights
Avoidance	When a person cannot face a situation effectively or does not have the skills to resolve the conflict situation successfully
Behaviour	A way of acting or responding
Blaming	It is your fault! Making others responsible for my situation
Body language	Information given by posture or motion as opposed to words
Budget	A plan according to which you make, use and save money
Busyness	Keeping oneself busy without necessarily being productive
Cognitive	A process that involves thinking and reasoning
Collaborating	Working through tough feelings to find a mutually satisfying solution for a problem
Commitment	To bind oneself to a cause or promise
Competencies	Abilities or skills
Compromise	Both sides give up something in order to gain something
Confrontation	Facing conflicting issues or persons
Congruent	Aligned or compatible
Connection and cohesion	Making contact with others and maintaining close, meaningful or trusting relationships
Consensual validation	Mutual agreement; more than one person sees it in the same light
Consensus	A general agreement by everyone; staying with that part of the proposal on which everyone has agreed
Constructive discontent	Being unsatisfied to the point of doing something positive about it
Creative thinking	Thinking out of the box, non-conforming
Criticism	Act of judging or giving an opinion
Cultural awareness	Awareness of other's way of living and doing things

Delaying tactics	Strategies aimed at underplaying or cooling off the situation
Delay of gratification	To wait to satisfy a want; postponing impulsive reactions in order to respond appropriately
Democracy	Majority rules
De-role	By telling others that they can be themselves again and that they can let go of the negative emotions or the roles they have played
Discrimination	Make a distinction; it can also mean that you treat a person differently, or as an inferior
Dreams	Subconscious thoughts usually occurring during sleep; also future visions
Egocentric	Self-centred, selfish and based on personal needs and viewpoints
Emotional competencies	Personal and interpersonal competencies that are important for personal satisfaction, relationships and career advancement and leadership
Emotional intelligence	The ability to identify, name and process emotions and use them as a source of information and to connect and empathize with others
Emotional processing	Process of dealing with emotions with the aim of understanding them and learning useful lessons
Empathy	To identify with the experiences of others
Energy levels	Degree to which a person can actively take part; level of energy available to the person
Equal opportunities	Ground rules, the art of listening, giving respectful feedback, no interrupting, looking for mutually acceptable solutions, keeping to the structure of the process and joint planning
Ethnocentric	Relating to the culture and traditions of a race or tribe
Etiquette	Polite manners, conventional rules of behaviour in polite society
Extroverted	Lively, sociable personality
Fear	Unpleasant feeling caused by impending danger or pain
Financial freedom	To be in control of your finances and provide for events unforeseen and the future in general
Flow	Being joyfully absorbed in a task or process that you are so comfortable with, interested in, and capable of doing, that you momentarily lose your sense of time passing; you experience the process as spontaneous and almost effortless
Forgiveness	Very powerful emotional skill, and is particularly relevant in mental health; highly resilient people do not bear grudges
Frame of reference	Viewpoint based on a person's experience, upbringing and belief system
Goals	Aims of someone's ambition
Group conformity	To be part of a group with specific norms and values
Habits	Settled inclination or trend of mind; patterns of behaviour
Impulse control	Resisting the temptation to act immediately
Inquisitive mindset	A tendency to question situations and things
Interdependent	Groups or individuals depending on each other
Internal locus of control	Controlling and motivating yourself as opposed to being controlled by others or circumstances
Intrapersonal skills	The skills of understanding and managing oneself
Intrapreneurship	As employee you take responsibility for the productivity and financial viability of a particular department, which functions as a profit centre

Introverted	The tendency to be shy or quiet or to keep to oneself
Invincible	People who function well despite adversity
Job specific	Related to work content, and to a specific job
Learning point	A fact or the focus of the learning exercise
Life balance	To balance different aspects of one's life
Logical thinking	Reasoning, analysing and thinking in sequence or in an organized manner
Mastery	To reach a very high level of competency – to be very good at it
Meaning	Having significance or deeper spiritual value
Metaphors	A comparison or figure of speech
Name-calling	Lazy-bones! Liar! Thief! Attaching certain attributes to others
Negative emotions	Feelings of discomfort, disapproval, rejection and alienation
Negotiation	Creates opportunities for both sides to win; the objective of negotiation is to resolve the conflict with a mutually satisfying agreement
Non-assertive people	Fail to express their feelings, thoughts and beliefs and act submissively
Optimism	To be confident and inclined to cheerfulness and a positive outlook
Ownership	To take personal responsibility for something
Paradoxical traits	Contradicting or opposing mannerisms, habits or personality characteristics
Paraphrasing	Putting or reformulating another person's statements or remarks in your own words to check for understanding
Personal empowerment	Being confident, informed and equipped to deal with a variety of issues
Personal identity	Being sure of who you are and what you stand for
Personal value system	Set of beliefs and values that guides the emotions and actions of the individual
Polycentric	Centred around other people and their needs as opposed to being self-centred
Potency	Strength or power of influence
Power play	The misuse of power to put another person at a disadvantage for your own benefit; it involves either using forceful tactics to make someone submit to your demands or withholding something another person wants or needs and thereby disempowering the other person – you could use your position of status, privileged information, or physical force
Prejudice	Adverse judgements or opinions formed without factual verification, based on assumptions
Prioritizing	Arranging issues or tasks according to their importance
Private space	Enough space to work in, apart from each other, so that individuals sit on their own, without interference from others
Pro-activity	Anticipating future trends and making provision for them; preparing in advance
Procrastinating	Putting things off until later; delaying action
Productivity	To create, invent, and produce on time
Punctual	To be on time, to do things according to plan
Racism	The belief that human races have distinctive characteristics that make some races superior and so have the right to rule over other races
Resilience	Successful adaptation to risk and adversity and life in general to live a fulfilling, happy life

Resourceful	Having a good, full 'toolkit' of techniques and adapting and responding to circumstances
Respect	Show politeness, kindness and positive regard
Responsible	To have a personal duty towards; to be personally accountable for
Self-acceptance	To appreciate myself and I am committed to myself as I am
Self-actualization	Experiencing life fully, vividly, selflessly, with full concentration and total absorption to become the best you can be
Self-appreciation	To appreciate and value yourself
Self-assessment	Looking at oneself critically to make a judgement
Self-concept	The idea one has of oneself as a person – physically and mentally
Self-confidence	Belief in my ability to deal with life
Self-disclosure	Sharing information about oneself with others
Self-esteem	My rating of myself
Self-knowledge	Understanding myself – my personality, talents and shortcomings
Self-management	Taking control of myself, my time, my emotions and my actions
Self-motivation	Encouraging myself to move forward
Self-reflection	Thinking about oneself and analysing oneself
Self-respect	Appreciating, valuing and feeling positive about myself
Self-responsibility	Taking responsibility for my life and my actions
Self-sufficiency	Being confident about my ability to handle my life, my challenges and to be able to fulfil my needs
Sexism	The assumption that one sex is superior, and therefore has the right to define the other sex's role in society
Solitude	Loneliness and seclusion; being on one's own
Stereotypes	A way of categorizing people – for example of a certain gender, race, religion or career – as being exactly the same
Strokes	Acknowledging something about another person, and giving feedback to that person; strokes can be negative or positive – negative strokes are criticism, positive strokes are compliments
Submissive	Shy, undemanding
Suppress	To overpower
Synergy	To act together in a mutually beneficial way – the end result is more than the sum of the inputs
Tabula rasa	Empty or blank slates – like a clean page, ready to be written on
Time-wasters	Activities that are unproductive
Transferable or functional skills	Skills needed in most work situations, normally taught at school, and include reading, writing and arithmetic
Vision	Foresight – a dream of the future
WIN message	W stands for When, and describes a specific behaviour or action; I stands for 'I' messages and explains how the sender feels; N stands for the negative result of the behaviour

Bibliography

Adair, John (1997) *Effective Communication*, London: Macmillan

Alder, Harry (1999) *The Right Brain Manager*, London: Judy Piatkus (Publishers)

Anderson, Nancy (1994) *Work with Passion: How to Do What You Love for a Living*, Novato, CA: New World Library

Anderson, Walter (1997) *The Confidence Course: Seven Steps to Self-Fulfillment*, New York: HarperCollins

Applewhite, Ashton (1995) *Thinking Positive: Words of Inspiration, Encouragement and Validation for People with AIDS and Those Who Care for Them*, London: Simon & Schuster

Barker, Larry L. and Gaut, Deborah A. (1996) *Communication*, New York: Simon & Schuster

Bays, Brandon (1999) *The Journey*, London: Thorsons

Bernard, B. (1992) 'Peer programs: a major strategy for fostering resilience in kids', *The Peer Facilitator Quarterly*, 9, 3

Blanchard, Ken and Johnson, Spencer (2004) *The One Minute Manager*, London: HarperCollins Busines

Borysenko, Joan and Borysenko, Moroslav (1994) *The Power of the Mind to Heal*, Carlsbad, CA: Hay House

Bovée Courtland, L. and Thill, John V. (1992) *Business Communication Today* Third Edition, New York: McGraw-Hill

Branden, Nathaniel (1994) *The Six Pillars of Self-Esteem*, New York: Bantam Books

Brown, Joseph (1982) *The Spiritual Legacy of the American Indian*, New York: Crossroad Publishing

Burns, Robert (1988) *Coping with Stress*, Cape Town: Maskew Miller Longman

Canfield, Jack and Hansen, Mark Victor (eds) (2000) *Chicken Soup for the Soul*, London: Vermilion

Carlson, Richard (1999) *Don't Sweat the Small Stuff Workbook*, London: Hodder & Stoughton

Cava, Roberta (1990) *Dealing with Difficult People*, London: Judy Piatkus (Publishers)

Chopra, Deepak (1996) *Creating Health*, London: Thorsons

Cohen, Bernice (1999) *Financial Freedom*, London: Orion Business Books

Cooper, Robert and Sawaf, Ayman (1998) *Emotional Intelligence in Business: Executive EQ*, London: Orion Business Books

Cousins, Norman (1979) *Anatomy of an Illness as Perceived by the Patient: Reflections on Healing and Regeneration*, New York: Bantam

Covey, Stephen R. (1994) *The Seven Habits of Highly Effective People*, London: Simon & Schuster

Covey, Stephen R. (1997) *The Seven Habits of Highly Effective Families*, London: Simon & Schuster

Crane, Thomas G. (2000) *The Heart of Coaching*, San Francisco, CA: FTA Press

Crum, Thomas (1987) *The Magic of Conflict*, London: Simon & Schuster

Csikszentmihalyi, Mihaly (1990) *Flow: The Psychology of Optimal Experience*, London: HarperCollins

De Bono, Edward (1985) *Conflicts: A Better Way to Resolve Them*, London: Penguin

Dobson, James C. (1998) *Solid Answers: America's Foremost Family Counselor Responds to Tough Questions Facing Today's Families*, Wheaton, IL: Tynedale House

Dryden, Gordon and Vos, Jeannette (1994) *The Learning Revolution – The life-long learning programme for the world's finest computer, your amazing brain*, Aylesbury, Bucks: Accelerated Learning Systems

Dyer, Wayne W. (1976) *Your Erroneous Zones*, London: Warner Books

Edmonds, R. (1986) 'Characteristics of effective schools', in U. Neisser (ed.) *The School Achievement of Minority Children: New Perspectives*, Hillsdale, NJ: Lawrence Erlbaum

Fourie, Louis and Codrington, Graeme with Grant-Marshall, Sue (2002) *Mind Over Money*, Parklands, South Africa: Penguin Books

Friedman, M. and Rosenbaum, R. H. (1974) *Type A Behaviour and Your Heart*, New York: Fawcet Crest

Fromm, Erich (1956) *The Art of Loving*, London: HarperCollins

Gardner, Howard (1983) *Frames of Mind*, New York: Basic Books

Garmezy, N. (1985) 'Stress-resistant children: the search for protective factors', in J. E. Stevenson (ed.) *Recent Research in Developmental Psychopathology*, Oxford: Pergamon Press

Garmezy, N. and Rutter, M. (eds) (1983) *Stress, Coping, and Development in Children*, New York: McGraw-Hill

Gawain, Shakti (1978) *Creative Visualization*, Novato, CQ: New World Library

Gawain, Shakti (1997) *The Four Levels of Healing: A Guide to Balancing the Spiritual, Mental, Emotional, and Physical Aspects of Life*, Mill Valley, CA: Narataj Publishing

Gibran, Kahlil (1955) *The Prophet*, Kingswood, Surrey: Windmill Press

Goleman, Daniel (1998) *Working with Emotional Intelligence*, London: Bloomsbury

Gray, John (1999) *How to Get What You Want and Want What You Have*, London: Random House

Gray, John (2002) *What You Feel You Can Heal*, Heart Publishing

Grovè, Shani (1996) *Thank You, Brain*, Cape Town, South Africa: Human & Rousseau

Grovè, Shani (2003) *Think Light*, Pretoria, South Africa: Litera Publications

Grulke, Wolfgang with Silber, Gus (2000) *Ten Lessons from the Future*, Parklands, Souith Africa: @One Communications

Hanks, Kurt (1991) *Motivating People: How to Motivate Others to do What You Want, and Thank You for the Opportunity*, Menlo Park, CA: Crisp Publications

Heystek, Magnus (1995) *World of Money: Don't Say You haven't been Warned!*, South Africa: Cream Publishers

His Holiness the Dalai Lama (2001) *The Art of Living: A Guide to Contentment*, Joy and Fulfillment, London: Thorsons

Holt, John (1994) *How Children Fail*, London: Pitman

Honig, Leonie (1996) *How to Raise Emotionally Intelligent Children*, South Africa: Smile Education

Humphreys, Tony (1996) *The Family – Love it and Leave it*, Dublin: Colourbooks

IBM (1994) *Working Smarter: The Learner Within*, IBM Corporation E.I.S.C.

Jawarski, Joseph (1996) *Synchronicity: The Inner Path of Leadership*, San Francisco: Berrett-Koehler

Kehoe, John (1994) *A Vision of Power and Glory*, West Vancouver, British Columbia: Zoetic

Kindler, Herbert, S. (1993) *Managing the Technical Professional*, Menlo Park, CA: Crisp Publications

Kiyosaki, Robert T. with Lechter, Sharon (1998) *Rich Dad, Poor Dad*, New York: Warner Books

Knight, Sue (1995) *Neuro Linguistic Programming at Work*, London: Nicholas Brealey Publishing

Kübler Ross, Elizabeth (1997) *On Death and Dying*, New York: Touchstone

Luft, Joseph (1963) *Group Processes: An Introduction to Group Dynamics*, Mayfield Publishing Company. Reprinted (1994) in *Experiential Learning Activities: Individual Development*, NY: Pfeiffer & Company

Manning, Matthew (2002) *The Healing Journey*, London: Judy Piatkus (Publishers)

Maslow, Abraham H. (1954) *Motivation and Personality*, New York: Harper and Row

Masuda, M. and Holmes, T. (1978) 'Life events: perceptions and frequencies', *Psychosomatic Medicine*, 40, 3, 236–61

McArdle, Geri E. H. (1995) *Managing Differences*, Menlo Park, CA: Crisp Publications

McWilliams, J. and Roger, John (1990) *You Can't Afford the Luxury of a Negative Thought – A book for people with any life-treatening illness including life*, London: Thorson

Millman, Dan (1998) *The Twelve Gateways to Human Potential*, London: Hodder & Stoughton

Mindpower (1994) *Explore Your Inner Self*, London: Timelife Books, Dorling Kindersley

Mindpower (1995) *Dare to be Yourself*, London: Timelife Books, Dorling Kindersley

Mindpower (1996a) *Develop Your Positive Energies*, London: Timelife Books, Dorling Kindersley

Mindpower (1996b) *Take Control of Your Life*, London: Timelife Books, Dorling Kindersley

Moore, Thomas (1992) *Care of the Soul*, New York: HarperCollins

Orman, Suze (1999) *The Courage to Be Rich*, New York: Riverhead Books

Peck, M. Scott (1978) *The Road Less Travelled*, London: Simon & Schuster

Perls, Thomas T. and Hutter Silver, Margery (1999) *Living to be 100*, New York: Basic Books

Pert, Candace B. (1997) *Molecules of Emotion*, London: Simon & Schuster

Peters, Thomas and Waterman, Robert (1982) *In Search of Excellence*, New York: Harper and Row

Phillips, Maya (1997) *Emotional Excellence: A Course in Self-Mastery*, New York: Element Books

Pienaar, W. and Spoelstra, M. (1992) *Negotiation: Theories, Strategies and Skills*, Cape Town: Juta Academic

Pikes, T., Burrell, B. and Holliday, C. (1998) 'Using academic strategies to build resilience', *Reaching Today's Youth*, 2, 3, 44–7

Radke-Yarrow, M. and Brown, E. (1993) 'Resilience and vulnerability in children of multiple-risk families', *Development and Psychopathology*, 5, 581–92

Reich, Robert (1991) *The Work of Nations,* New York: Alfred Knopf

Rifkin, J. (1995) *The End of Work: The decline of the global labor force and the dawn of the post market era*, New York: Jeremy Tarcher

Robbins, Anthony (1992) *Awaken the Giant Within: How to Take Immediate Control of Your Mental, Emotional, Physical and Financial Destiny*, London: Simon & Schuster

Robert, M. (1982) *Managing Conflict From The Inside Out*, New York: Pfeiffer

Rooth, Edna (1995) *Lifeskills: A Resource Book for Facilitators*, Manzini, Swaziland: Macmillan Boleswa Publishers

Ruiz, Don Miguel (1952) *The Four Agreements: Practical Guide to Personal Freedom*, San Rafael, CA: Amber-Allen Publications

Ruskan, John (1998) *Emotional Clearing*, London: Rider Books (Random House)

Rutter, M. (1987) 'Psychosocial resilience and protective mechanisms', *American Journal of Orthopsychiatry*, 57, 3

Ryback, David (1998) *Putting Emotional Intelligence to Work: Successful leadership is more than IQ*, Boston: Butterworth Heinemann

Schrank, Louise Welsh (1991) *How to Choose the Right Career*, Lincoln Wood, IL: VGM Career Horizon

Seligman, Martin E.P. (1990) *Learned Optimism: How to Change Your Mind and Your Life*, New York: Pocket Books

Senge, Peter M. (1992) *The Fifth Discipline: The Art and Practice of the Learning Organisation*, New York: Doubleday

Siebert, Al (1996) *The Survivor Personality*, New York: Perigee Books (Berkley)

Siegel, Bernie (1990) *Peace, Love and Healing*, London: Rider Books

Smith, Jane (1997) *How to be a better … Time Manager*, London: Kogan Page

Smith, Manual J. (1975) *When I Say No, I Feel Guilty*, London: Bantam Double Day Publishing

Smith Wasmer, Linda (1997) *Focus of Mind and Body*, New York: Henry Holt

Steiner, Claude with Perry, Paul (1997) *Achieving Emotional Literacy*, London: Bloomsbury

Temoshok, L. and Dreher, H. (1992) *The Type C Connection: The Mind–Body Link to Cancer and Your Health*, New York: Plume

Vaillant, George (1993) *The Wisdom of the Ego*, Cambridge, MA: Harvard University Press

Volpe, Renate (2000) *The Entrepreneurial Mindshift*, Goodwood: Print 24

White, Randall P., Hodgson, Philip and Crainer, Stuart (1996) *The Future of Leadership*, London: Pitman

Wilks, Frances (1998) *Intelligent Emotion*, London: Heinemann

Wismer, Jack N. (1994) *A Communication-Skills Practice*, San Diego, CA: Pfeiffer and Company

Yogananda, Paramahansa (1994) *Sayings of Paramahansa Yogananda, 4th edition*, Los Angeles: Self-Realization Fellowship

Appendix: The National Curriculum – alignment with PSHE and Citizenship

The following table aligns PSHE (Personal, Social and Health Education) and Citizenship outcomes with *Resilience* Volumes 1 and 2 learning material.

Developing confidence and responsibility and making the most of their abilities		
PSHE and Citizenship outcomes	**Resilience Volumes 1 and 2**	
Children should be taught:	**Unit**	**Activity Sheet**
a) to talk and write about their opinions and to explain their views on issues that affect themselves and society.	My world (vol 1) Diversity (vol 2)	3 1, 5, 6
b) to recognize their worth as individuals by identifying positive things about themselves and their achievements, seeing their mistakes, making amends and setting personal goals.	Resilience (vol 1) Marvellous me (vol 1) My time (vol 1)	1, 2, 3, 4, 7, 8, 9, 10 1, 2, 3, 7, 8 2, 3, 4, 5, 6, 7, 8, 9, 10, 11, 12
c) to face new challenges positively by collecting information, looking for help, making responsible choices and taking action.	Finding solutions (vol 2) Moving on (vol 2)	1, 2, 3, 4, 5, 6, 7, 8, 9, 10, 11 1, 2, 3, 4, 5, 6, 7, 8, 9, 10
d) about the range of jobs carried out by people they know and to understand how they can develop skills to make their own contribution to the future.	Money matters (vol 2)	1, 11
e) to look after their money and realize that future wants and needs may be met through saving.	Money matters (vol 2)	1, 2, 3, 4, 5, 6, 7, 8, 9, 10, 12

Preparing to play an active role as citizens		
PSHE and Citizenship outcomes	**Resilience Volumes 1 and 2**	
Children should be taught:	**Unit**	**Activity Sheet**
a) to research, discuss and debate topical issues, problems and events.	Diversity (vol 2)	1, 2, 5
b) why and how rules and laws are made and enforced, why different rules are needed in different situations and how to take part in making and changing rules	Diversity (vol 2)	5
c) to realize the consequences of antisocial behaviours, such as bullying and racism, on individuals and communities.	Emotions (vol 1)	5, 7

	Empathy (vol 2)	4
	Finding solutions	9
d) that there are different kinds of responsibilities, rights and duties at home, at school and in the community and that these can sometimes conflict with each other.	My time (vol 1)	2, 3, 4, 5, 6, 7
	Finding solutions (vol 2)	5, 6, 7
e) to reflect on spiritual, moral, social and cultural issues, using imagination to understand other people's experiences.	My world (vol 1)	1, 7
	Diversity (vol 2)	1, 2, 3, 4, 6, 7
f) to resolve differences by looking at alternatives, making decisions and explaining choices.	Conflict (vol 2)	1, 2, 3, 4, 5, 6, 7, 8, 9, 10, 11, 12, 13, 14
g) what democracy is, and about basic institutions that support it locally and nationally.	Diversity (vol 2)	5, 6
h) to recognize the role of voluntary, community and pressure groups.	Diversity (vol 2)	5
i) to appreciate the range of national, regional, religious and ethnic identities in the United Kingdom.	My world (vol 1)	2, 4, 6
j) that resources can be allocated in different ways and that these economic choices affect individuals, communities and the sustainability of the environment.	Diversity (vol 2)	1, 2
k) to explore how the media present information.	Free to be me (vol 1)	1, 2
	Conflict (vol 2)	8

Developing good relationships and respecting the differences between people		
PSHE and Citizenship outcomes	**Resilience Volumes 1 and 2**	
Children should be taught:	**Unit**	**Activity Sheet**
a) to realize that their actions affect themselves and others, to care about other people's feelings and to try to see things from other people's point of view.	Emotions (vol 1)	1, 2, 3, 4, 5, 6
	Free to be me (vol 1)	3, 4, 5, 6, 7, 8, 9, 10, 11
	My world (vol 1)	1, 2, 3
	Empathy (vol 2)	1, 2, 3, 4, 5, 6, 7, 8, 9, 10, 11, 12

		Finding solutions (vol 2)	5, 6, 10
		Conflict (vol 2)	6, 7, 8, 9, 10
b)	to think about the lives of people living in other places and times, and people with different values and customs.	Resilience (vol 1)	5
		My world (vol 1)	1, 2, 3, 4, 5, 6, 7
		Diversity (vol 2)	1, 2, 3, 4, 5, 6, 7
c)	to be aware of different types of relationship, including marriage and those between friends and families, and to develop the skills to be effective in relationships.	Resilience (vol 1)	6, 7, 12
		Marvellous me (vol 1)	2, 5
		Emotions (vol 1)	6, 7, 8
		Empathy (vol 2)	3, 4, 6, 7, 8, 9, 10, 11
d)	to realize the nature and consequences of racism, teasing, bullying and aggressive behaviours, and how to respond to them and ask for help.	Emotions (vol 1)	7, 8
		Finding solutions (vol 2)	9, 11
e)	to recognize and challenge stereotypes.	My world (vol 1)	1, 2, 4, 5, 6, 7
f)	that differences and similarities between people arise from a number of factors, including cultural, ethnic, racial and religious diversity, gender and disability.	My world (vol 1)	1, 4, 5, 6, 7
g)	where individuals, families and groups can get help and support.	Finding solutions (vol 2)	11

Although *Resilience* Volumes 1 and 2 were designed and developed to comply with/conform to/augment Key Stage 2 PSHE guidelines, both volumes offer learning opportunities for Key Stage 3 and 4 PSHE topics. For example:

Key Stage 4 Outcomes

Developing confidence and responsibility and making the most of their abilities	
Outcome	Resilience Volumes 1 and 2
Children should be taught:	Unit
a) to assess their strengths in relation to personality, work and leisure	Resilience (vol 1)

		Marvellous me (vol 1) My time (vol 1)
b)	to respect differences between people, developing their own sense of identity	Resilience (vol 1) Marvellous me (vol 1) My world (vol 1) Diversity (vol 2)
c)	to recognize how others see them, give and receive constructive feedback	Resilience (vol 1) Marvellous me (vol 1) My world (vol 1) Empathy (vol 2) Conflict (vol 2)
d)	to be aware of emotions associated with loss and change caused by death, divorce, separation and new family members	Emotions (vol 1) Finding solutions (vol 2) Moving on (vol 2)
e)	to think about personal qualifications and skills, choices at Key Stage 4, the changing world of work	Money matters (vol 2)
f)	to think about targets for Key Stage 4, seeking out help with career plans	—
g)	to realize influences on spending, managing personal money	Money matters (vol 2)

Developing good relationships and respecting the differences between people	
PSHE and Citizenship outcomes	**Resilience Volumes 1 and 2**
Children should be taught:	**Unit**
a) to recognize stereotyping, prejudice, bullying, racism and discrimination	My world (vol 1) Empathy (vol 2)

b) to empathize with people different from themselves	My world (vol 1) Diversity (vol 2) Empathy (vol 2) Free to be me (vol 1)
c) to reflect on the nature of friendship	Free to be me (vol 1) Empathy (vol 2)
d) to think about cultural norms in society, lifestyles and relationships	My world (vol 1) Diversity (vol 2)
e) to be aware of the changes in, and pressure on relationships with friends and family	Finding solutions (vol 2) Moving on (vol 2)
f) to recognize the role and importance of marriage in family relationships	My world (vol 1)
g) to recognize the role and feelings of parents and carers, the value of family life	Marvellous me (vol 1) Empathy (vol 2)
h) to be aware that goodwill is essential to positive relationships	Empathy (vol 2) Free to be me (vol 1) Conflict (vol 2)
i) to negotiate within relationships, when and how to make compromises	Conflict (vol 2) Empathy (vol 2)
j) to resist pressures to do wrong	—
k) communicate confidently with peers and adults	Free to be me (vol 1) Conflict (vol 2)